Just feed me

THIS SIGNED EDITION HAS BEEN SPECIALLY BOUND BY THE PUBLISHER

Just feed me

ALSO BY JESSIE JAMES DECKER

Just Jessie

Just feed me

SIMPLY DELICIOUS RECIPES FROM MY HEART TO YOUR PLATE

Jessie James Decker

DEY ST.

An Imprint of WILLIAM MORROW

HarperCollins books may be purchased for educational, business, or sales promotional use. For information, please email the Special Markets Department at SPsales@harpercollins.com.

FIRST EDITION

Designed by Michelle Crowe
White marble background by Patty Chan/ Shutterstock, Inc.

Library of Congress Cataloging-in-Publication Data has been applied for.

ISBN 978-0-06-294820-5

20 21 22 23 24   LSC   10 9 8 7 6 5 4 3 2 1

I want to dedicate this book to my hubby and babies for loving their mama's cookin' so much and encouraging me to try new things and loving them.

Some of my favorite memories and moments are in the kitchen cookin' with a baby on my hip or one of them sittin' on the island tasting the cookie dough or sneakin' samples. Here's to many more memories and delicious meals to be made together.

And, of course, I must dedicate this book to my fans who inspired me to put out a cookbook. Without y'all's support and encouragement, I would have never written this. Your love and excitement for food bring us even closer. Enjoy these recipes, and I can't wait to see what your favorites are!

Contents

Introduction

I come from a long line of strong Italian cooks. My mama taught me how to cook, her mama taught her how to cook, and she learned from her mama, my great-grandmother, and so on.

But though our roots are Italian, my upbringing was Southern and Cajun. I have fine memories of the smell of garlic on my great-grandmother Maw Maw Mary's hands, and waking up to homemade pancakes my grandmother Gee Gee would make when we stayed at her house, or the countless nights my mama would make Cajun white beans and rice or fry off some catfish or make her famous pumpkin Bundt cake. We hardly ever ate out growing up. Mama always cooked and my love for home-cooked meals was instilled in me early on.

Today, I share that love with my family. I cook for them every day—and I love every minute of it. I make a little espresso, put on my French cooking music, start the olive oil and garlic in the pan, wait for it to become fragrant, and I am completely in my element.

Hopefully, what you'll love about my cookbook is how easy these recipes are. I am not a chef, nor do I pretend to be. What I am is a prideful home cook, and what I would like for y'all to take from this book is that you can be, too.

There is nothing more fulfilling than seeing your husband take a bite of something you made for dinner and make that "mmmm" noise, or seeing your babies finish their bowls of pasta and being so satisfied to know their little bodies are growing strong and they are getting all the nourishment they need from something you created. Life can be busy and get a little hectic, but when it comes to food, I don't skimp. Dinner especially is a time to create delicious meals and sit around the dining table together enjoying fresh food, a glass of wine, and conversation.

Because we're all busy people—I get it, y'all!—I've also included a bunch of "quick feeds," recipes that you can make to feed your babies in 20 minutes or less. Your hubby is sure to love them, too!

I like to say I grew up a "gypsy," living in and traveling to many different cities and states, and that I took a little something with me every time we left. Each place where we lived had a special dish that I kept as a memory and now cook in my kitchen. The many recipes I will share range from the meals I learned from my mama to the restaurant dishes that I've enjoyed and then decided to play the guessing game on how to make—

ultimately coming up with my own versions. You'll also get my recipes for meals I've had to pull together last minute—the babies were hungry—using things I had on hand, like the vegetables in the fridge and the cans in the pantry. So many of these "of necessity" recipes come out great. You will see many dishes inspired by my Italian and Cajun roots, plus healthy sweets and Tex-Mex dishes I've fallen in love with from my childhood and my travels as an adult.

I'm an eater, and always have been. My love for food only gets stronger and stronger. So y'all enjoy my very first cookbook, and I hope to spread the love of cooking from my kitchen to yours and the three simple words that cut right to the chase: just feed me.

SOME TIPS, SUPPLIES, AND THOUGHTS ABOUT COOKING

This book is my own personal collection of foods, recipes, and tricks I've picked up along the way to make cooking enjoyable, easy, and simply delicious. There are a few things that I have in the kitchen all the time, from cooking utensils to ingredients. You will always find these in my kitchen:

Cooking Supplies

* Baking sheets
* Blender
* Cake pan
* Cake stand
* Can opener
* Casserole dish

* Cheese grater
* Cutting boards
* Dutch oven
* Measuring spoons and cups
* Meat/candy thermometer
* Muffin tins

* Parchment paper
* Pizza pan
* Roasting pan
* Rolling pin

* Shellfish cracker
* Stand mixer or hand mixer
* Wooden platters
* Wooden spoons

Staples

Here are some things I always have in my fridge and/or pantry for quick shortcut meals for a hungry family!

In the fridge or freezer

* Garlic, fresh and jar of minced in the fridge
* Frozen jasmine rice
* Block of Parmesan cheese

* Pancetta
* Pork sausage
* Frozen bell pepper
* Frozen onion

In the pantry

* Olive oil
* Cajun seasoning
* Ro-tel mild diced tomatoes and green chilies
* Canned kidney beans

* Canned green beans
* Canned mushrooms
* Canned olives
* Spaghetti

Why these items? Well, I can think of at least five meals right now that I could throw together with some of these ingredients. When the babies are hungry and you haven't had time to run to the grocery store, these items can become handy real quick.

Things to throw together quickly

* *shortcut cacio e pepe:* spaghetti, pancetta, garlic, olive oil, Parm, and salt and pepper

* *shortcut jambalaya:* pork sausage, jasmine rice, Ro-tel mild diced tomatoes and green chilies, and bell pepper all in a pan with Cajun seasoning

* *easy pasta and sausage dish:* spaghetti, sausage, bell pepper, olive oil, and seasoning

* *simple sausage and rice dish:* in a pan, bake sliced pork sausage, green beans, onions, bell pepper, and garlic and serve over rice

* *quick snack or appetizer:* put a can of olives in a small serving dish and add salt, pepper, and garlic

But First, Y'all, Breakfast and Brunch

Breakfast and I have an "anything goes" kind of relationship. There are mornings I want a big breakfast with chocolate chip pancakes, bacon, and eggs, and other mornings I'm happy with a slice of toast with butter alongside my coffee. But if anyone knows me, they know I won't skip it no matter what time of day it is. It just feels wrong to me. Even if it's one o'clock and I haven't eaten because I've been working and time got away from me, I will still have a croissant or a breakfast bar before I have that sandwich or salad at lunch. I know it's odd, but it's just my own little strange thing I've done since I was little.

When I was a kid, sometimes my mama would throw Pillsbury orange cinnamon rolls in the oven and fry up some bacon and I was the happiest kid ever. There are still those moments I will pop the same Pillsbury cinnamon rolls in the oven and get my kids just as excited as I was, cutting them in half and hearing them discuss whether the center or the outside of the cinnamon roll is the best part. It's the start of a good morning, because food is conversation. I just love everything about breakfast.

Extra-Fluffy Homemade Pancakes

There have been many secret nights when Eric and I are lying in bed at 9 p.m., the babies sound asleep, and we just give each other that look with smirks.

"Pancakes?!" we say at the same time with a laugh, and then we'll run like small children into the kitchen to get started. He's been in the habit of grabbing the Bisquick, but I wanted to create our own recipe for the number of nights we do this. These are the fluffiest pancakes in the world and will have you making that "mmmm" noise with every melted butter and syrup bite.

MAKES 5 TO 7 PANCAKES

prep time: 5 MINUTES   *cook time:* 10 MINUTES

1 cup all-purpose flour

2 tablespoons sugar

2 teaspoons baking powder

Pinch of salt

1 large egg, beaten until frothy

1 cup buttermilk

2 tablespoons unsalted butter, melted and cooled, plus more for the skillet and for serving

1 tablespoon pure vanilla extract

Pure maple syrup, for serving

Chocolate chips, for serving (optional)

IN a medium bowl, whisk together the flour, sugar, baking powder, and salt. In a small bowl, beat the egg, buttermilk, melted butter, and vanilla. Add the egg mixture to the dry ingredients and mix well.

HEAT a skillet over medium-low heat and add butter to melt. Pour the batter into the pan and cook for 2 to 3 minutes, or until the air bubbles begin to burst. Flip and cook the other side for 1 to 2 minutes, just until lightly browned. Transfer to a plate and cover to keep warm.

REPEAT with the rest of the batter and more butter as needed to make more pancakes.

SERVE with butter and syrup or top with chocolate chips, if desired.

Oatmeal Bake with Blueberry Syrup

This dish is like dessert. My kids love oatmeal as much as I do, so I wanted to create something that spruced it up a little bit.

MAKES 6 SERVINGS

prep time: 10 MINUTES   *cook time:* 35 MINUTES

FOR THE OATMEAL

1 teaspoon coconut oil, melted, for the baking dish

2 cups old-fashioned rolled oats

½ teaspoon baking powder

½ teaspoon ground cinnamon

1 cup unsweetened applesauce

2 large eggs

½ cup unsweetened vanilla almond milk

2 tablespoons creamy almond butter, melted

2 tablespoons pure maple syrup

1 teaspoon pure vanilla extract

1 cup blueberries

FOR THE BLUEBERRY SYRUP

½ cup blueberries

1 tablespoon pure maple syrup

make the oatmeal: Preheat the oven to 350°F. Grease an 8 x 6-inch glass baking dish with the coconut oil.

IN a large bowl, stir together the oats, baking powder, and cinnamon. Add the applesauce, eggs, almond milk, almond butter, maple syrup, and vanilla and mix until just combined. Fold in the blueberries. Pour into the prepared baking dish and spread evenly.

BAKE until the top is golden brown, 30 to 35 minutes.

meanwhile, make the blueberry syrup: In a small saucepan, combine the blueberries and maple syrup and bring to a boil over medium heat. Reduce to a simmer and cook until the blueberries can be mashed easily with the back of a spoon, about 10 minutes. Set aside to cool.

ONCE the oatmeal bake is cooked, cut into 6 pieces and drizzle with the blueberry syrup.

Fancy Scrambled Eggs

We have scrambled eggs most days, so once in a while we like to switch it up. Scrambled eggs are very easy to make, so this recipe just adds a little something to your breakfast to give it some color and extra flavor. Serve with a side of toast and butter and sliced avocado.

MAKES 1 OR 2 SERVINGS

prep time: 5 MINUTES   *cook time:* 10 MINUTES

6 large eggs

2 tablespoons whole milk

2 to 3 tablespoons olive oil, plus more for drizzling

Salt and freshly ground black pepper

2 cups arugula

1 cup tricolor cherry tomatoes, sliced

CRACK your eggs into a medium bowl and add the milk. Whisk it up real good.

IN a skillet, heat a good amount of oil until it's so hot you hear it sizzle. Pour your eggs into the hot pan and let the edges fry a little. Once the center is almost set, after about 3 to 4 minutes, use a silicone spatula to fold it over.

ONCE it's done, which will take another minute, season with salt and pepper and put it on a plate as one serving or divide the eggs into two servings. Grab the arugula and sprinkle it on top of the eggs. Next add the colorful sliced tomatoes. Drizzle the whole thing with a little oil and season with more salt and pepper.

Colombian Calentado

This was one of the last meals I had before giving birth to my third baby, Forrest. We flew back to Colorado because I love and trust my doctor there so much. We stayed in a hotel in Englewood, Colorado, and of course I was hungry and wanted to have my last big meal before going in to deliver Forrest. We stopped at this cute little Colombian coffee shop nearby, and on the menu I saw "Colombian Calentado" and the description of eggs, rice, beans, and bacon, and I was convinced.

It was so good that I never forgot it and decided I needed it again. After Forrest was born, we came back to Nashville and I created this recipe from memory. This is an extra-special dish to me, as I will always remember it as my last meal before having my sweet baby boy.

MAKE 3 OR 4 SERVINGS

prep time: 5 MINUTES   *cook time:* 15 MINUTES

2 Roma (plum) tomatoes, diced

2 tablespoons chopped scallions

¼ teaspoon garlic powder

¼ teaspoon ground cumin

Olive oil, for drizzling

Salt and freshly ground black pepper

2 cups cooked white or brown rice, at room temperature or chilled

1 (15.5-ounce) can red beans, rinsed and drained

3 or 4 fried eggs (1 per serving)

6 or 8 slices thick-cut bacon (2 per serving)

IN a small saucepan, combine the tomatoes, scallions, garlic powder, cumin, and a drizzle of oil (about ½ tablespoon). Season with salt and pepper to taste and cook over medium-low heat until the tomatoes soften, about 15 minutes. Add the rice and beans and cook, stirring gently until heated through.

TO serve, scoop a helping of the bean and rice mixture onto a plate, top each serving with a fried egg, and add the bacon on the side.

note

Calentado, *which means "heated" in Spanish, is a traditional Colombian breakfast made of reheated leftovers of rice and beans.*

Hawaiian Roll Breakfast Sandwiches

When I bring the Hawaiian rolls home from the grocery store and Eric spots them in the bag, his eyes light up and a big smile appears, because he knows breakfast sandwiches are on the menu for the week.

These are so simple but so delicious and filling—they are one of Eric's favorite breakfasts that I make him. The crunchy bite on the bacon and the melted butter dripping down the warm rolls will have you grabbing for thirds.

MAKES 12 SERVINGS

prep time: 10 MINUTES   *cook time:* 20 MINUTES

FOR THE EGGS

About 3 tablespoons olive oil

5 large eggs

2 tablespoons whole milk

Salt and freshly ground black pepper

FOR THE ROLLS

¾ pound bacon

1 (12-count) package Hawaiian rolls

3 tablespoons unsalted butter, melted

2 to 4 tablespoons mayonnaise

make the eggs: In a skillet, drizzle in a good amount of oil (I like to practically deep-fry the eggs) and set the pan over medium heat.

IN a medium bowl, whisk the eggs with the milk until light.

WHEN the oil is hot, put the beaten eggs into the skillet and watch them sizzle and fry, but don't touch them. You want them to stay flat and in one piece.

FRY scrambled eggs for 5 minutes, or until the edges are set, then flip the eggs with a spatula (it doesn't have to be perfect) and season with salt and pepper to taste. Cook for an additional minute. Remove from the heat and cover while you prepare the bacon and rolls.

assemble the rolls: In a large skillet, fry the bacon over medium-high heat until the strips are browned on the bottom, about 4 minutes. Flip with tongs and cook for an additional 2 minutes, or until browned and crispy. Lay flat on paper towels to drain while you assemble the rolls.

SLIGHTLY toast the Hawaiian rolls with a layer of butter on top. Simply slice the sheet of Hawaiian rolls open and brush the butter on the cut sides. Then brown in a toaster oven or under a hot broiler for a good 3 minutes.

SPREAD 2 tablespoons mayonnaise over the bottom buns, then top with the egg and then the bacon. Finish with another layer of mayo on the top bun, if desired, so it all sticks together, and sandwich them together. That's it!

Ham and Sweet Potato Hash

I hosted a cooking competition in Nashville a few years back with some pretty big chefs. They were told to do a Chopped-style cook-off with the minimal ingredients they were given. One of the chefs whipped up this breakfast ham and sweet potato hash and I still to this day remember holding the mic while salivating, trying to keep my hosting duties professional when all I wanted to do was steal a taste.

I decided to add it to the family menu and make it at home immediately. It's now a family favorite and great when hosting guests.

MAKES 4 SERVINGS

prep time: 10 MINUTES   *cook time:* 20 MINUTES

2 medium sweet potatoes, peeled and diced

½ teaspoon Cajun seasoning

¼ teaspoon salt

¼ teaspoon freshly ground black pepper

2 tablespoons olive oil, plus more for frying the eggs

1 cup diced yellow onion

1 cup diced thick-cut ham

4 large eggs

1 tablespoon chopped fresh parsley, for garnish

IN a medium bowl, toss together the sweet potatoes, Cajun seasoning, salt, and pepper.

IN a cast-iron skillet, heat the oil over medium heat. Add the onion and sweet potato and cook until tender, about 10 minutes.

ADD the diced ham to the skillet and stir frequently until heated through, about 5 minutes. While the hash is cooking, in another skillet, heat some oil and fry the eggs to everyone's liking.

SERVE each portion of hash with a fried egg on top and garnish with the parsley.

Buttermilk Cinnamon Rolls

When I was pregnant with Vivi, this was one of my requests daily (which is maybe why I gained fifty-five pounds with her).

MAKES 12 ROLLS

prep time: 2 HOURS   *cook time:* 25 MINUTES

FOR THE DOUGH

¼ cup warm water

5 tablespoons plus 1 teaspoon granulated sugar

1 envelope active dry yeast

3 tablespoons unsalted butter, melted and cooled

1 cup buttermilk, room temperature

4 cups all-purpose flour, plus more for the dough

Pinch of salt

1 large egg, lightly beaten, at room temperature

2 teaspoons vegetable oil

FOR THE FILLING

3 to 4 tablespoons unsalted butter, melted and cooled

½ cup packed light brown sugar

2 tablespoons ground cinnamon

make the dough: In a small bowl, mix the lukewarm water, 1 teaspoon of the granulated sugar, and the yeast and set aside to proof for just a few minutes.

IN a stand mixer with the dough hook (or in a large bowl by hand), combine the melted butter, the remaining 5 tablespoons granulated sugar, the yeast mixture, and buttermilk. With the mixer on low, beat in 2 cups of the flour and the salt (or stir it in by hand).

ADD the egg and continue to mix, then add the remaining 2 cups flour. Turn the dough out onto a lightly floured surface and knead. If the dough is too wet, add a little more flour 1 tablespoon at a time.

ONCE the dough is soft and elastic, form into a ball and place in a lightly oiled bowl. Cover and let rise in a warm, dark area until doubled in size, about 1 hour.

DUMP the risen dough onto a work surface and gently form it into a rectangle roughly ½ inch thick.

prepare the filling: Brush the dough with the melted butter and sprinkle generously with the brown sugar and cinnamon.

ROLL the dough tightly into a log and cut crosswise into ½-inch slices. Place the slices, cut side up, into a large cast-iron skillet or square baking dish. Cover loosely with a towel and let rise for another 30 minutes.

AFTER about 20 minutes of rising, start preheating the oven to 375°F.

FOR THE ICING

1 (8-ounce) block cream cheese, at room temperature

2 tablespoons unsalted butter, at room temperature

½ cup powdered sugar

½ teaspoon almond extract

Pinch of salt

1 to 2 tablespoons whole milk

TRANSFER the rolls to the oven and bake until browned, about 25 minutes, checking after 10 to 15 minutes for browning. If the rolls are browning too quickly, cover loosely with foil and continue to bake. Let the rolls rest for about 10 minutes.

meanwhile, make the icing: In a large bowl, with an electric mixer, beat the cream cheese, butter, powdered sugar, almond extract, and salt until smooth. Beat in enough milk to thin to a spreadable consistency. Refrigerate until ready to use.

SPREAD the icing on the rolls before serving.

Breakfast Sausage Balls

This might be my favorite breakfast food of all the recipes, which is funny because it's so simple. I always mimic my version of Joey from Friends *during the Thanksgiving episode: "meat, good, bread, good, cheese, GOOD." Rub some butter or jam on them and watch them all disappear.*

MAKES 10 SERVINGS

1 pound bulk sausage

1 pound sharp Cheddar cheese, shredded

2 cups baking mix, such as Jiffy or Bisquick

Melted butter, for dipping

prep time: 15 MINUTES   *cook time:* 30 MINUTES

PREHEAT the oven to 350°F. Line a large baking pan with foil.

IN a large bowl, mix the ground sausage and Cheddar until well combined (see Tip). Add the baking mix and continue to mix until there are no dry lumps left. It will look a little dry, but don't overmix!

ROLL into medium-size balls (you will get about 20 balls). Arrange in the prepared pan and bake until golden, 20 to 30 minutes. Serve with melted butter for dipping!

tip

Getting all the ingredients to mix is easiest when everything is at room temperature, so set out your cheese and sausage for about 20 minutes before you're ready to make these balls.

Fried Breakfast Tacos

I am a huge lover of Tex-Mex and will find any way to eat it daily, so why not include it in my breakfast? I fry up the tacos the same way I do my dinner tacos. The fried tortillas really make these special.

MAKES 4 TO 6 SERVINGS

prep time: 10 MINUTES *cook time:* 15 MINUTES

4 to 6 large eggs

2 tablespoons whole milk

Salt and freshly ground black pepper

Olive oil, for frying the eggs and tortillas

4 to 6 slices thick-cut bacon

4 to 6 fajita-size flour tortillas

Sliced avocado, for serving

Shredded Mexican cheese blend, for serving

Louisiana hot sauce, for serving

IN a medium bowl, whisk the eggs with the milk. Season with salt and pepper.

IN a large nonstick skillet, heat a drizzle of oil over medium heat. Add the eggs and scramble until they are firm and no liquid egg remains, about 5 minutes. Transfer the eggs to a plate.

IN the same skillet over medium-high heat, cook the bacon until the strips are browned on the bottom, about 4 minutes. Flip with tongs and cook for an additional 2 minutes, or until browned and crispy. Transfer to a plate lined with paper towels.

IN a separate large skillet, heat 3 to 4 tablespoons oil over medium-high heat. Add 1 tortilla at a time, frying each side for 3 to 5 seconds. Transfer to a plate lined with paper towels and repeat.

TO assemble each taco, layer a tortilla with a scoop of egg and a slice of bacon down the middle. Top with sliced avocado, shredded Mexican cheese, and a couple squirts of Louisiana hot sauce. Fold over and enjoy.

The Good Stuff
Before the Main Stuff

We all need a little somethin' somethin' before the main thing, right? That's what I love about appetizers. I never skip apps, because they really get the taste buds and belly warmed up for the main thing. I like to make sure the apps all go together with whatever style of food I'm cooking. For example, if I'm making Italian, I always put out a cheese and meat tray. Or if I'm doing tacos, I like to have my nachos or Eric's guac and margaritas all set up before the main course. When I'm having people over or hosting a get-together, I always have appetizers out to keep people satisfied while the main meal is in the works. Here are some of my appetizer go-tos.

Fried Goat Cheese with Mango Salsa

One of my favorite restaurants in the entire world is Tommy Bahama. They have this fabulous goat cheese and mango salsa appetizer with crackers that I salivate over as soon as I sit down and they hand me my menu (which they don't really need to do since I know that menu from top to bottom). I love it so much, but I needed to figure out how to make it in my own kitchen for when I can't make it into Tommy's.

MAKES 8 SERVINGS

prep time: 20 MINUTES   *cook time:* 10 MINUTES

½ cup salted roasted macadamia nuts, roughly chopped

10 ounces good-quality goat cheese

8 tablespoons (1 stick) unsalted butter, melted

Mango Salsa (recipe follows)

½ cup Sweet Soy Glaze (recipe follows)

White corn tortilla chips or butter crackers, for serving

FILL a shallow bowl with the chopped macadamia nuts. Divide the goat cheese into 4 equal portions and roll into balls, then roll each in the chopped macadamia nuts, pressing the nuts in gently to cover the sides. Flatten each ball into a round, then coat in macadamia nuts again, to cover any newly exposed goat cheese.

IN a large nonstick skillet, heat the butter over medium heat. Add the goat cheese rounds and fry for about 1 minute on each side.

GARNISH with the mango salsa and soy glaze and serve with tortilla chips or crackers.

Mango Salsa

MAKES 2 CUPS

1½ cups diced mango

2 strips red bell pepper, petite diced

2 tablespoons chopped scallions

½ tablespoon minced jalapeño

1 tablespoon fresh lime juice

1 tablespoon extra-virgin olive oil

Salt and freshly ground black pepper

IN a small bowl, stir together the mango, bell pepper, scallions, jalapeño, lime juice, oil, and salt and pepper to taste.

REFRIGERATE to let the flavors combine.

Sweet Soy Glaze

MAKES ABOUT 1¼ CUPS

1 cup soy sauce

1½ cups sugar

1 tablespoon olive oil

¼ teaspoon seeded and minced jalapeño

IN a small saucepan, combine the soy sauce, sugar, oil, and jalapeño and cook over medium high-heat until the sauce begins to thicken, about 20 minutes. Strain the sauce to remove any bits of jalapeño left, then let cool.

Eric's Easy Guacamole

I never knew how much I loved avocado until I became an adult. Avocados were very expensive when I was younger and we couldn't afford them, so I never even tried guacamole until I was in my early twenties.

In the beginning of my relationship with Eric he told me he didn't cook much but he could make some mean guacamole, and boy was he right! He's so cute with the guacamole bowl, mashing all the ingredients with his sweet smile all proud. But I will tell you that after he's done mixing up all the ingredients (when he's not looking) I like to sneak in some spices just to flavor it up a bit. He doesn't know I do this, but he will now when he reads this cookbook! Ha!

MAKES 8 TO 10 SERVINGS

4 avocados, diced

⅓ cup diced red onion

2 tablespoons roughly chopped fresh cilantro

Juice of 1 lime

½ teaspoon garlic powder

Salt and freshly cracked black pepper

Tortilla chips, for serving

prep time: 5 MINUTES

IN a bowl, mash the diced avocado with a fork, leaving it somewhat chunky. You can also use a mortar and pestle. Add the onion, cilantro, lime juice, and garlic powder and stir to combine. Season with salt and pepper to taste and serve with tortilla chips.

Shrimp Mango Ceviche

I love shrimp, I love avocado, and I love mango. So what's not to love about this shrimp mango ceviche, right? This dish is so fresh and flavorful, and it's the perfect thing to serve when having guests over for a summer gathering. Put this in a pretty serving bowl next to a colorful bowl of tortilla chips and watch people fight over the last bite.

MAKES 6 TO 8 SERVINGS

prep time: 20 MINUTES   *cook time:* 12 MINUTES

1 pound shrimp, peeled, deveined, and chopped

Salt and freshly ground black pepper

¼ cup fresh lime juice (2 to 3 limes), plus more to taste

1 small or ½ large mango, chopped

1 small avocado, cut into chunks

½ medium red bell pepper, chopped

¼ cup diced red onion

1 cup halved multicolored grape tomatoes

1 medium cucumber, diced

2 tablespoons torn fresh cilantro

2 tablespoons avocado oil

White corn tortilla chips, for serving

BRING a large soup pot of water to a boil over high heat.

IN a small bowl, season the shrimp with salt and pepper to taste and toss to coat. Add the shrimp to the boiling water and once they turn pink, about 2 minutes, transfer to a large colander and run under cold water. Slice the shrimp in half crosswise and transfer to a medium bowl. Add the ¼ cup lime juice, toss to coat, and let that sit and cool.

IN a large bowl, combine the mango, shrimp, avocado, bell pepper, red onion, tomatoes, cucumber, and cilantro and toss to combine. Season with salt and lime juice to taste and drizzle with the oil.

LET stand at room temperature for a minimum of 15 minutes for the flavors to settle. Serve with white corn tortilla chips.

Peanut Butter Bacon

OK, I know y'all are thinking this one sounds weird, but I promise it's not. If you love peanut butter and you love bacon, then this is your recipe, honey. I had this app at my favorite steak house in New York City and I was hooked. I knew I needed this in my life at all times, not just when I travel to the Big Apple. The thick bacon with peanut butter and the jalapeño jelly all together make for a uniquely delicious starter that could possibly outshine the main course.

MAKES 8 SERVINGS

prep time: 10 MINUTES *cook time:* 15 MINUTES

2 cups sugar

2 sticks (8 ounces) unsalted butter

1 cup heavy cream

2 tablespoons shiro miso paste

2 cups unsalted dry roasted peanuts

4 slices thick-cut bacon, halved crosswise

2 to 3 tablespoons store-bought apple-jalapeño jelly

1 jalapeño, thinly sliced

IN a large saucepan, combine the sugar, butter, and ½ cup of the cream and bring to a boil over medium-high heat. Reduce the heat to medium and cook, stirring constantly, until it browns and a thick caramel forms, 5 to 7 minutes. Remove from the heat and whisk in the remaining ½ cup cream and the miso.

IN a food processor, puree the peanuts until the texture of chunky peanut butter and fold into the cooled caramel.

PAN-FRY the bacon over medium-high heat until the strips are browned on the bottom, about 4 minutes. Flip with tongs and cook for an additional 2 minutes, or until browned and crispy. Transfer to a plate lined with paper towels.

TO serve, spoon a dollop of peanut butter caramel onto a plate and layer with the bacon and apple-jalapeño jelly. Top with a slice of fresh jalapeño.

THE GOOD STUFF BEFORE THE MAIN STUFF

Roasted Cauliflower and Red Pepper Dip

Eric and I flew to Minnesota a while back and stopped in to see Mike, his best friend from his hometown. Mike's wife, Shelly, and I both were pregnant at the same time and I was so excited to see her and talk about our growing bellies. When we arrived, she had made an incredible meal that I'll never forget.

We sat out on their back porch as the boys stood over the grill cooking steaks. One of the appetizers she had out on the table was a grilled cauliflower with this homemade dip. I had never had it before, and I fell in love with it immediately. I loved it so much she inspired me to make something very similar. This is great to put out when having guests.

MAKES 4 TO 6 SERVINGS

prep time: 10 MINUTES   *cook time:* 50 MINUTES

2 roasted red peppers (from a 12-ounce jar)

½ cup almonds

1 small clove garlic, peeled

1 tablespoon sherry vinegar

Salt and freshly cracked black pepper

¼ cup olive oil

1 medium-to-large head cauliflower, trimmed

IN a food processor, combine the roasted red peppers, almonds, garlic, vinegar, and a sprinkle of salt and pepper and pulse to combine. With the machine running, stream in 3 tablespoons of the oil and process into a thick paste perfect for dipping. Taste and adjust the salt and pepper if needed!

PREHEAT the oven to 425°F. Line a baking pan with foil.

PLACE the head of cauliflower in the prepared baking pan and brush with the remaining 1 tablespoon oil. Season with salt and pepper. Roast the cauliflower until tender, 30 to 50 minutes depending on the size. To brown, place the pan under a hot broiler until crisp.

ONCE finished, let cool and serve with the fancy dip.

tip

If you have an outdoor grill, I recommend putting the cauliflower on the grill to char and cook. Heat the grill to 400°F and prepare the cauliflower according to the recipe. Place a large piece of foil on the grill grates and add the cauliflower. Grill until tender and the edges begin to char, about 40 minutes.

THE GOOD STUFF BEFORE THE MAIN STUFF

Chicken Meatballs

These chicken meatballs are something I threw together spontaneously one afternoon. I had some ground chicken I needed to use in the refrigerator so I went into the pantry to see what I could create and I saw my Italian bread crumbs. I typically use my Italian bread crumbs for chicken Parm, but that day I figured I would try them in meatballs to see how they would turn out.

I made a smallish batch (I was saving some of the ground chicken for a pasta dinner that night), but the meatballs were such a hit that the kids and Eric ate them up quickly and immediately wanted more. So I had to pull the rest of the ground chicken out of the refrigerator and quickly make more meatballs! These are perfect in Tuscan White Bean Soup (page 69) or as an appetizer with dipping sauce.

MAKES 35 MEATBALLS

prep time: 5 MINUTES   *cook time:* 40 MINUTES

2 pounds ground chicken

1 tablespoon Italian seasoning

1 teaspoon garlic powder

1 teaspoon Tony Chachere's Creole Seasoning

Salt and freshly ground black pepper

1 cup Italian-style bread crumbs

Olive oil, for frying

IN a large bowl, season the chicken with the Italian seasoning, garlic powder, Tony's seasoning, and salt and pepper to taste. Use your hands to mix everything together. Add the Italian bread crumbs and mix until combined. Roll into 35 balls about the size of golf balls (about 1½ tablespoons).

HEAT a large heavy skillet over medium heat for 1 minute. Pour in enough oil to cover the bottom and let it get hot.

WORKING in batches of 10 to 12, fry the meatballs, shaking the pan so they don't stick and turning with tongs as they brown. Cook until they are completely browned, 7 to 10 minutes. You can slice one open to test for doneness.

They Don't Call Me Salad Queen for Nothin'

I never knew how much I loved salads until I became an adult. When I was a kid, we didn't do many salads, and if I ever had one, it was iceberg lettuce and ranch dressing from the cafeteria. EWWY! as my kids say. The more I ventured out, went to new restaurants, or had a friend make something in her kitchen, I realized salads are the best!

I started getting creative, and it began with a bag of arugula and some freshly grated Parmesan cheese. A girlfriend of mine threw a little salad together at her house back in the day using only olive oil and lemon juice and it was so good. I took that idea and created my own dressing.

Once I got comfortable with my arugula, homemade salad dressing, and freshly grated Parmesan, I added my seasoning—garlic powder, salt, and pepper. From there I would throw in olives and sliced vegetables. I even got really wild and tossed in greens from different lettuce families and also fruits.

It was a habit that I had no plan on breaking. I had become a salad-aholic and would be forever. Here are some of my go-to salads that I make in my home weekly. I probably have a hundred more recipes I could share, but I will start with these for now! Get yo green on y'all!

Homemade Go-To Salad Dressing

I use this dressing on pretty much every salad with maybe a few variations. I like it because it's light, easy, and goes with any salad recipe you can dream of. If you don't always keep fresh lemons in the house like I do, store some lemon juice in your fridge so you can always whip this up.

MAKES ½ CUP

¼ cup olive oil

3 tablespoons balsamic vinegar

Juice of 1 lemon

½ teaspoon garlic powder

Salt and freshly ground black pepper

prep time: 5 MINUTES

IN a screw-top jar or salad dressing shaker, combine the oil, vinegar, lemon juice, garlic powder, and salt and pepper to taste. Shake well! Taste and adjust the seasoning to your preference. That's it! Very simple.

Butter Lettuce Salad

My husband loves apples more than anyone I know. You can always count on him to have at least one apple a day. The man never gets sick so there may be something to that old wives' tale. Because of his love of apples, I try to incorporate this favorite fruit into whatever recipe I can think of. He particularly loves apples in his salads, so I created this delicious butter lettuce, goat cheese, and apple salad for my sweet hubby to enjoy. When he catches me slicing the apples and sees the big wooden bowl and tongs on the counter, his eyes light up because he knows this salad is coming.

MAKES 2 TO 3 SERVINGS

prep time: 5 MINUTES

FOR THE VINAIGRETTE

¼ cup olive oil

3 tablespoons sherry vinegar

Juice of 1 lemon

½ teaspoon garlic powder

Salt and freshly ground black pepper

FOR THE SALAD

1 to 2 heads butter lettuce, leaves torn

1 Honeycrisp or Gala apple, peeled and thinly sliced

2 ounces goat cheese, crumbled

2 tablespoons slivered almonds

Salt and freshly ground black pepper

make the vinaigrette: In a screw-top jar or salad shaker, combine the oil, vinegar, lemon juice, garlic powder, and salt and pepper to taste. Shake well.

assemble the salad: Layer a large bowl or serving dish with lettuce leaves and dress with the vinaigrette. Top with the apple slices, goat cheese, and almonds. Season with salt and pepper to taste before serving.

Arugula, Goat Cheese, and Couscous Salad

Right before Eric the second was born, while we were living in New Jersey, I decided to plan ahead and have some easy premade meals ready to go since I am the only cook in the house. I did as much research as possible because I wanted to eat home-cooked meals while having to do as little as possible. I like takeout, but only once in a blue moon. I got completely spoiled by my mother making homemade meals my entire childhood. So, after many Google searches, I decided that the fresh meal kits—where everything is laid out for you and you just cook it up— were the way to go.

I knew I would be breastfeeding my newborn and I would be extremely hungry and wanting easy, quick meals. One of those meal kits had a version of this recipe, which is how I found my love for couscous, arugula, and goat cheese. Nine out of ten times I'll also grill up some salt and pepper lemon chicken to lay on top of this delicious salad.

MAKES 4 TO 6 SERVINGS

prep time: 15 MINUTES   *cook time:* 30 MINUTES

1 cup pearl couscous

4 tablespoons olive oil

1 small red onion, cut into thin rings

1 zucchini, sliced into ½-inch rounds or half-moons

Kosher salt and freshly ground black pepper

¼ cup fresh lemon juice

2 tablespoons chopped fresh parsley

1 teaspoon white wine vinegar

1 cup baby arugula

8 ounces goat cheese, chilled and crumbled

COOK the pearl couscous according to the package directions. Set aside in a large bowl.

IN a small skillet, heat 2 tablespoons of the oil over low heat. Add the onion and cook until caramelized, about 20 minutes.

MEANWHILE, preheat the broiler.

ON a sheet pan, toss the zucchini with the remaining 2 tablespoons oil and a pinch each of salt and pepper. Slide under the broiler and broil until cooked through and charred slightly, about 5 minutes.

ADD the zucchini and onion to the cooked couscous. Add the lemon juice, parsley, vinegar, arugula, goat cheese, and some salt and pepper and toss to fully combine before serving.

Arugula, Bacon, and Pine Nut Salad

One of my sister Sydney's favorite things that I make are my salads, especially this one. She gets so excited when I tell her there will be a salad with dinner. To be honest, I get a lot of phone calls from my sister or my brother-in-law Anthony asking what's for dinner. Sometimes they won't even tell me if they're coming over or not—they will just show up at the door and say I heard you were making . . . I always make plenty of food, so the more the merrier.

My sweet baby girl Vivi is allergic to a lot of nuts and seeds, so this one in particular excites her because she also loves salads and she can have the pine nuts; between those pine nuts and the crunch of the bacon, that first bite is full of so much flavor!

MAKES 2 SERVINGS

prep time: 5 MINUTES   *cook time:* 10 MINUTES

FOR THE BACON VINAIGRETTE

2 slices center-cut bacon
1½ tablespoons apple cider vinegar
1½ teaspoons light brown sugar
1½ teaspoons Dijon mustard
2 teaspoons onion powder
⅛ teaspoon dried basil
⅛ teaspoon dried oregano
⅛ teaspoon dried rosemary
⅛ teaspoon dried thyme
Pinch of ground turmeric
Salt and freshly ground black pepper

FOR THE SALAD

1 (5-ounce) bag baby arugula
2 to 3 tablespoons pine nuts
Freshly grated Parmesan, for serving

make the bacon vinaigrette: In a medium skillet over medium-high heat, cook the bacon until the strips are browned on the bottom, about 4 minutes. Flip with tongs and cook for an additional 2 minutes, or until browned and crispy. Transfer to a plate lined with paper towels. When the bacon is cool enough to handle, crumble it.

WHILE the bacon drippings in the pan are still warm, add the vinegar, brown sugar, mustard, onion powder, dried herbs, turmeric, and salt and pepper to taste. Whisk everything together, then stir in the bacon.

assemble the salad: Place the arugula in a large bowl, drizzle with the dressing, add the pine nuts, and toss everything together. Finish off with freshly grated Parmesan before serving.

Caprese Salad

During the warm Tennessee summers this is my favorite salad to eat. I get so excited picking the fresh basil leaves from the herb garden Eric planted for me. I immediately smell the fresh picked leaves and smile. It's one of my favorite scents. Eric will pour us some fabulous red wine and we will share one plate of this salad and fight over who gets the last bite.

MAKES 4 SERVINGS

1 (8-ounce) ball fresh mozzarella, sliced

1 cup sliced grape tomatoes

Sea salt and freshly cracked black pepper

8 to 10 fresh basil leaves

3 to 4 tablespoons balsamic glaze (from Trader Joe's)

1 tablespoon olive oil

prep time: 5 MINUTES

ARRANGE the mozzarella and tomatoes on a plate or platter. Season with sea salt and cracked black pepper to taste. Top with the basil leaves and drizzle with the balsamic glaze and oil before serving.

Peach Caprese Salad

My favorite fruit in the whole world is peaches. I fell in love with peaches early on, but I grew even more in love with them when we lived in Georgia and my parents would take us peach picking. Just like in the movie Forrest Gump *when Bubba Gump shares his love of shrimp, that's my love of peaches. I love peaches in this salad, I love peach cobbler, I love peach pie, peach crisp, peach ice cream, peaches on my pancakes, peach jam . . . the list can go on.*

This peach caprese salad will definitely impress your guests when they see the beautiful presentation of prosciutto alongside the fresh peaches. Top it off with freshly ground pepper and a pinch of salt.

MAKES 4 SERVINGS

prep time: 10 MINUTES

8 ounces mozzarella cheese, sliced

2 peaches, sliced

1 cup sliced tricolor grape tomatoes

2 ounces prosciutto, thinly sliced

2 to 3 tablespoons olive oil

2 tablespoons balsamic vinegar

Salt and freshly ground black pepper

6 to 8 fresh basil leaves

LAYER the mozzarella, peaches, tomatoes, and prosciutto on a large platter. Drizzle with the oil and vinegar. Season with salt and pepper and top with fresh basil before serving.

Mixed Green Avocado Salad

This mixed green avocado salad is fresh and delicious with every crunch of a Kalamata olive and avocado bite. I love to top it off with grilled shrimp and freshly squeezed lemon.

MAKES 2 MAIN-COURSE SERVINGS OR 4 SIDES

prep time: **10 MINUTES**

FOR THE VINAIGRETTE

¼ cup avocado oil

3 tablespoons balsamic vinegar

Juice of 1 lemon

½ teaspoon garlic powder

Salt and freshly ground black pepper

FOR THE SALAD

1 medium cucumber, sliced

1 avocado, diced

¼ medium red onion, sliced

½ cup Kalamata olives, pitted and halved

4 cups spring salad mix

4 ounces feta cheese, cubed or crumbled

Salt and freshly ground black pepper

make the vinaigrette: In a screw-top jar or salad shaker, combine the oil, vinegar, lemon juice, garlic powder, and salt and pepper to taste. Shake well.

assemble the salad: In a large serving bowl, layer the cucumber, avocado, red onion, and olives over the spring mix. Dress with the vinaigrette, top with the feta, and toss to coat. Season with salt and pepper to taste before serving.

Grilled Watermelon Salad Pizza

This unique salad will be one of the most flavorful you've ever had. The juiciness of the watermelon running down your chin topped with prosciutto and sliced Parmesan will have you wondering if you want to even share. I can eat an entire watermelon salad pizza by myself. Just ask Eric.

MAKES 4 TO 6 SERVINGS

prep time: 5 MINUTES   *cook time:* 6 MINUTES

1 disk seedless watermelon, 1 to 2 inches thick

Salt and freshly ground black pepper

6 thin slices prosciutto

10 to 12 thin slices Parmigiano-Reggiano cheese

1 cup tricolor baby tomatoes, sliced

Handful of baby arugula

Balsamic glaze (from Trader Joe's), for garnish

PREHEAT an outdoor grill or cast-iron grill pan. Once hot, place the watermelon disk down on the grill to caramelize and mark, 2 to 3 minutes. With tongs or a large spatula, flip the watermelon and grill another 2 to 3 minutes. Remove the watermelon to a cutting board and let rest for about 5 minutes.

SEASON the grilled watermelon with salt and pepper. Top with the prosciutto, Parmigiano, tomatoes, and arugula and garnish with balsamic glaze.

SLICE into 6 to 8 "pizza" wedges and serve.

Warm-Me-Up Soups

Between soup and pasta, I can always come up with something. There are no wrong or right ingredients when creating a soup recipe. My family in particular loves when I have soup on the menu that day. They love the warm broth and hearty bits with every spoonful and slurp as they pick up their bowl with both hands, sipping the last bit of yummy juice as it runs down their little chins.

There was one week straight that my middle baby boy, Eric, asked for my chicken and rice soup every day even for breakfast. He's so darn pretty I almost gave in, but I stuck with oatmeal for breakfast and gave him more soup that night.

Chicken Noodle Soup

The classic chicken noodle soup. Everyone has their own chicken noodle soup, but I like to think mine is slightly different from your average bowl. For one, I add corn, and for another, I like to use spaghetti instead of egg noodles.

My kids love this soup and I make it a lot during those cold winter months to bring a little warmth to their bellies.

MAKES 6 SERVINGS

prep time: 15 MINUTES   *cook time:* 1 HOUR

1 rotisserie chicken

1 tablespoon unsalted butter

2 tablespoons olive oil

1½ cups diced carrots

1½ cups diced celery

1 cup diced onion

2 quarts chicken broth

1 (12-ounce) bag frozen white corn kernels

6 ounces spaghetti

1 tablespoon Tony Chachere's Creole Seasoning (adjust to your taste)

2 teaspoons garlic powder, or to taste

1 teaspoon dried thyme

2 bay leaves

Salt and freshly ground black pepper

¼ cup chopped fresh parsley (if you don't have fresh on hand, you can use dried!)

Saltine crackers, for serving

SHRED the rotisserie chicken meat and discard the skin and bones. Set aside.

IN a large pot, melt the butter in the oil over medium heat until nice and warm. Toss in the carrots, celery, and onion and stir with a wooden spoon. Cook until the veggies start to get soft, about 5 minutes. Pour in the broth. Add the shredded chicken and frozen corn and let that cook while you prepare the noodles.

BRING a large pot of water to a boil over high heat. Snap the spaghetti in half, add to the boiling water, and cook until several minutes less than the time given on the package directions.

WHILE the pasta boils, season the soup with Tony's seasoning, the garlic powder, thyme, bay leaves, and salt and pepper to taste.

DRAIN the pasta and add to the soup along with the parsley. Let the soup simmer for a good 45 minutes. Discard the bay leaves. Serve with saltine crackers.

Shrimp Avocado Medicine Soup

This soup will make you feel like a new person. The soothing broth is made from just vegetables and water. If you don't want the shrimp, this soup is great by itself.

I suggest making a big ol' pot of this and eating it for a week, especially if you are trying to cure a cold. The sliced avocado and drizzle of olive oil on top make this whole green goddess soup come together.

MAKES 6 SERVINGS

prep time: 10 MINUTES   *cook time:* 20 MINUTES

1 tablespoon Himalayan pink salt

1 cup quinoa

2 cups broccoli florets

6 ounces green beans, ends trimmed

1 (12-ounce) bag frozen white corn kernels

1 cup minced celery

2 cups cauliflower florets

2 cups diced baby zucchini (about 4 baby zucchini)

2 pounds shrimp, peeled and deveined

1 teaspoon garlic powder

2 tablespoons olive oil, plus more for serving

Salt and freshly ground black pepper

¼ cup finely chopped fresh cilantro

1 avocado, sliced, for serving

IN a large pot, bring 7 cups water with the salt to a boil over high heat. Reduce the heat to medium-high and add the quinoa, broccoli, green beans, corn, celery, and cauliflower. Cook until they begin to soften, 4 to 5 minutes.

ADD the zucchini and shrimp to the pot and season with the garlic powder, oil, and salt and pepper to taste. Return to a boil, then reduce to medium and let the soup simmer until the shrimp are cooked through, 6 to 8 minutes.

SERVE garnished with the cilantro, avocado slices, and a drizzle of oil.

Chicken Wild Rice Soup

My hubby is from the North, and he told me how important chicken and wild rice soup was for him and his childhood. I decided to do my research and come up with my own version, and let me tell you, it was a hit! This is one of his favorite soups I make, and he always gets this little grin right before he says, "Babe, how about some of that wild rice soup?"

MAKES 4 TO 6 SERVINGS

prep time: 15 MINUTES   *cook time:* 30 MINUTES

4 tablespoons (½ stick) unsalted butter

¼ cup all-purpose flour

1 cup whole milk

1 cup half-and-half

¼ teaspoon garlic powder

¼ teaspoon Tony Chachere's Creole Seasoning

Salt and freshly ground black pepper

3 cloves garlic, minced

1 yellow onion, diced

2 cups diced baby carrots

3 stalks celery, sliced

6 cups chicken broth

1½ cups frozen wild rice medley, or cooked wild rice

1 rotisserie chicken, meat removed and shredded

2 cups thinly sliced mushrooms

2 tablespoons chopped fresh parsley

3 sprigs fresh rosemary

2 bay leaves

½ teaspoon dried thyme

Warm bread, for serving

IN a large saucepan, melt the butter over medium heat. Whisk in the flour and cook until lightly browned, about 1 minute. Whisk in the milk and half-and-half and cook, stirring constantly, until it thickens, 4 to 5 minutes. Season the roux with the garlic powder, Tony's seasoning, and salt and pepper to taste.

ADD the garlic, onion, carrots, celery, chicken broth, and wild rice to the pot and bring to a boil over high heat. Reduce the heat to medium-low and add the shredded chicken, mushrooms, parsley, rosemary, bay leaves, and thyme and simmer until all the flavors have come together, about 15 minutes.

DISCARD the bay leaves and rosemary stems and serve with warm bread.

Lentil Bacon Soup

I love lentils and I love bacon, so I decided to create a lentil soup that combined two of my favorite things and was also easy and delicious. Anything that starts with bacon in the pan, you just know is going to be good. This is an easy and hearty recipe that will have you craving it the next day for lunch.

MAKES 4 TO 6 SERVINGS

prep time: 10 MINUTES   *cook time:* 1 HOUR 15 MINUTES

1 pound bacon
1 cup sliced carrots
1 cup diced onion
1 cup diced celery
2 cloves garlic, minced
1½ cups green lentils
2 quarts chicken broth
¼ cup chopped fresh parsley
1 teaspoon garlic powder
Salt and freshly ground black pepper

IN a large pot or Dutch oven over medium-high heat, cook the bacon until the strips are browned on the bottom, about 4 minutes. Flip with tongs and cook for an additional 2 minutes, or until browned and crispy. Transfer the bacon to paper towels and leave the bacon grease in the pot.

ADD the carrots, onion, and celery to the pot and sauté over medium-low heat until the onion is translucent, about 5 minutes. Add the garlic to the pot and continue to cook for 1 to 2 minutes.

ADD the lentils, chicken broth, parsley, garlic powder, and salt and pepper to taste. Chop or crumble the bacon and add it to the pot. Bring to a simmer, cover, and cook, stirring occasionally, until the lentils are soft, about 1 hour. Season with more salt and pepper if desired before serving.

Tuscan White Bean Soup

I used to make this for Eric when we lived in Denver and it was just us. I'll be honest, I would buy this box soup kit that had all the dried vegetables and seasonings, and just add the bacon and broth. I always got creative and added my own touches like potato and fresh spinach.

We had it weekly it was so darn good, but sadly one day I learned it got discontinued. I was devastated, so I googled the heck out of it and found a picture of the back of the box with all the ingredients and decided to make it from scratch. I was successful and Eric will even tell me it's better than the box soup kit I learned it from. Thanks, babe. :)

MAKES 6 SERVINGS

prep time: 10 MINUTES   *cook time:* 35 MINUTES

3 slices bacon, chopped

2 tablespoons olive oil

2 small carrots, chopped

½ cup diced onion

1 medium potato, peeled and cubed

4 cups chicken broth

1 (15-ounce) can white navy beans, rinsed and drained

Salt and freshly ground black pepper

3 packed cups baby spinach

Freshly grated Parmesan cheese

IN a large pot or Dutch oven over medium-high heat, cook the bacon until the strips are browned on the bottom, about 4 minutes. Flip with tongs and cook for an additional 2 minutes, or until browned and crispy. Transfer the bacon to paper towels to drain, leaving the bacon grease in the pot.

ADD the carrots, onion, and potato to the pot and sauté over medium-low heat until the onion is translucent and the veggies begin to soften slightly, about 15 minutes.

POUR in the chicken broth, add the white beans, and season with salt and pepper to taste. Chop or crumble the bacon and add it to the pot. Bring to a simmer over medium heat and cook for 10 minutes to let the flavors develop. Reduce the heat to medium-low, stir in the baby spinach, and let it wilt, about 3 minutes.

LADLE into bowls and serve with Parmesan.

White Bean and Bacon Soup

It doesn't get more simple and delicious than this recipe. This is one of those "Oh crap, I didn't get groceries, the kids are starving, and I got nothing in the pantry" meals. All ya need is bacon and white beans and you can make this happen. It is so delicious that no one will know you whipped it up quickly and with little effort.

MAKES 6 TO 8 SERVINGS

prep time: 10 MINUTES   *cook time:* 1 HOUR 30 MINUTES

5 slices bacon

2 tablespoons olive oil

½ cup diced onion

2 cloves garlic, minced

1 cup chopped carrots

3 (15.5-ounce) cans white beans with their liquid

2 cups chicken broth

1 teaspoon salt

½ teaspoon freshly ground black pepper

Tony Chachere's Creole Seasoning

Cooked white rice, for serving

IN a large pot over medium-high heat, fry the bacon until the strips are browned on the bottom, about 4 minutes. Flip with tongs and cook for an additional 2 minutes, or until browned and crispy. Transfer the bacon to paper towels to drain, leaving the bacon grease in the pot.

ADD the onion, garlic, and carrots to the pot and sauté until soft. Add the white beans, chicken broth, salt, pepper, and Tony's seasoning to taste and simmer over medium-low heat for 1½ hours.

STIR in the cooked bacon and serve over white rice.

Ground Chicken Tuscan Soup

This is on the fancier side of the soup spectrum. You can serve it at a dinner party in pretty bowls with your best silverware if you want. It looks impressive. I fell in love with this soup at one of my go-to restaurants and decided to create my own version of it.

MAKES 4 TO 6 SERVINGS   *prep time:* **10 MINUTES**   *cook time:* **45 MINUTES**

2 tablespoons olive oil

1 pound lean ground chicken

1 medium yellow onion, diced

3 cloves garlic, minced

3 stalks celery, chopped

2 medium carrots, diced

4 large Yukon Gold potatoes, sliced

6 cups chicken broth

Salt and freshly ground black pepper

1 bunch kale, midribs and tough stems removed, leaves chopped

¾ cup half-and-half or heavy cream

Freshly grated Parmesan cheese, for serving

IN a large skillet, heat 1 tablespoon of the oil over medium heat. Add the chicken and cook until browned, 5 to 7 minutes. Remove to a plate or bowl and discard any drippings.

IN a large pot or Dutch oven, heat the remaining 1 tablespoon oil over medium heat. Add the onion, garlic, celery, and carrots and cook until they begin to soften, about 5 minutes. Add the potatoes, cooked chicken, broth, and salt and pepper to taste. Cook over medium heat until the potatoes are tender, about 20 minutes.

STIR in the kale and continue to cook just until the leaves soften, about 5 minutes. Add the half-and-half and simmer for an additional 5 minutes.

LADLE into bowls and serve with Parmesan.

Crab Bisque

I love me some crab bisque, and anytime it's on a menu at a restaurant I'm immediately drawn to it and am geared up to order, except for one little thing. I will always ask the server politely, "How much crabmeat are we talking?" I need to know it's not just pureed in there. I want a friendly amount of meat in my bisque or it's not right. So I decided to take matters into my own hands and create my own meaty crab bisque with delicious sherry and heavy cream.

MAKES 4 TO 6 SERVINGS

prep time: 10 MINUTES   *cook time:* 25 MINUTES

1 tablespoon olive oil

½ large onion, minced

3 cloves garlic, minced

3 tablespoons unsalted butter

3 tablespoons all-purpose flour

1 cup chicken broth, plus more as needed

1 pound crabmeat, chopped

1 cup sherry

2 cups heavy cream, plus more as needed

Salt and freshly ground black pepper

Chopped scallion (optional), for garnish

Croutons (optional), for garnish

IN a medium skillet, heat the oil over medium heat. Add the onion and garlic and sauté until tender, about 5 minutes.

IN a large pot, melt the butter with the flour and stir until smooth, about 3 minutes. Add the broth and give everything a stir until you have a smooth mixture, about 2 to 3 minutes. Stir the sautéed onion and garlic into the pot. (You can puree this mixture with an immersion blender for a smooth soup. If you like a chunky bisque, just leave the broth mixture as it is!)

ONCE the soup base is hot, stir in the crabmeat and sherry and let the flavors fuse together for a few minutes. Slowly stir in the heavy cream until fully incorporated, adjusting for consistency with a splash more broth or cream if needed.

PORTION into wide soup bowls and season with salt and black pepper to taste. If desired, garnish with scallions and croutons.

Pasta Stole My Heart

My love of pasta started as early as my first memories. I'm always ready for it and can think of a hundred different recipes. When I was a kid, I had my first bites of "gravy." Gravy isn't what you're thinking right now either. I'm not talking about the brown or white gravy you pour on your biscuits or mashed potatoes. I'm talking about Sicilian gravy like my great-grandmother would make and passed all the way down to my mama. It's a secret recipe that will die with us all, but my point of sharing this is I wanted to make sure y'all understand my love and passion for pasta.

I will share with you some recipes I created in my kitchen over the years. My babies squeal with excitement when I tell them I'm making spaghetti for dinner. I will ask them, "Do y'all want the kind with meat sauce or the kind with Parm and pancetta?" This is something I do frequently—I love to give the family choices for dinner and let them decide so they feel like they're a part of the dinner planning. I hope through sharing my pasta recipes that you come up with your own recipes over time or really home in on what you and your family enjoy best. Personally, I love and will eat them all!

Creamy Ground Chicken Pasta

quick
feeds

My creamy ground chicken pasta is a special recipe. What I like about it is I made it up on the fly (which is how so many of my recipes happen), but I also love it because it's a mix of Italian and Southern comfort. The creamy chicken and mushrooms are hearty and filling mixed with the spaghetti. It's a down-home meal, one of those I like to whip up after we've been traveling and are tired of restaurant food and just want that comfort after being away from home. This dish truly gives your belly that homey happy feeling.

MAKES 4 SERVINGS

prep time: 10 MINUTES   *cook time:* 15 MINUTES

Salt
10 ounces spaghetti
2 tablespoons olive oil
8 ounces pancetta, diced
1 cup chopped yellow onion
1 cup sliced button mushrooms
3 cloves garlic, minced
1 pound lean ground chicken
1 cup chicken broth
1 cup half-and-half
2 tablespoons all-purpose flour
Freshly ground black pepper
2 generous handfuls arugula
Freshly grated Parmesan cheese, for serving

IN a large pot of salted boiling water, cook the spaghetti noodles to al dente according to the package directions. Drain and set aside.

IN a large skillet, heat 1 tablespoon of the oil over medium heat. Add the pancetta, onion, and mushrooms and cook until fragrant, about 5 minutes. Add the garlic and continue to cook over medium-low heat for another minute, until the garlic begins to soften. Remove from the heat.

IN a separate skillet, heat the remaining 1 tablespoon oil over medium-high heat. Cook the ground chicken until browned, about 6 to 8 minutes, breaking it up with a wooden spoon or spatula. Add the cooked chicken to the onion/pancetta mixture and return the skillet to medium-high heat.

REDUCE the heat to medium. Add the broth, half-and-half, and flour and stir constantly to thicken, about 5 minutes. Season with pepper to taste. Fold in the drained pasta and the arugula.

SERVE hot with Parmesan.

Lemon Spinach Shrimp Pasta

This recipe is very light but flavorful. Vivi loves shrimp the most of all the meats and fishes, so she particularly loves this dish. If you're not in the mood for a heavy Bolognese, this is your go-to. Serve this with warm garlic bread.

MAKES 6 SERVINGS

prep time: 10 MINUTES   *cook time:* 15 MINUTES

Salt

1 pound spaghetti

2 pounds medium wild-caught shrimp (I prefer Gulf shrimp), peeled and deveined

3 to 4 tablespoons olive oil

3 cloves garlic, minced

1 cup baby tomatoes, halved

3 cups spinach

½ cup freshly grated Parmesan cheese, plus more for serving

Juice of 1 lemon

1 teaspoon crushed red pepper flakes

Freshly ground black pepper

IN a large pot of salted boiling water, cook the spaghetti until al dente according to the package directions. Drain and set aside.

IN a large skillet, heat 3 tablespoons of the oil over medium-high heat. Add the garlic and sauté just until fragrant, 2 to 3 minutes. Add the shrimp and cook over medium heat for 2 to 3 minutes, flip with tongs and cook for 2 to 3 more minutes, or until the shrimp is pink and slightly charred.

FOLD in the tomatoes, spinach, Parmesan, and drained spaghetti and continue to cook for an additional minute until heated through. Drizzle with the lemon juice and toss to coat. If the noodles seem too dry, add another 1 tablespoon oil.

SEASON with the pepper flakes and salt and black pepper to taste. Serve topped with Parmesan.

Lemon-Basil Pasta

This is another light pasta for those who want something fresh and flavorful but not too heavy. Eric started an herb garden for me, and my favorite is our basil plant. I use our fresh basil in the summer on anything and everything I can think of. I highly suggest that, if you can, you grow one or keep one in your kitchen. It just really makes the recipe.

MAKES 4 SERVINGS

prep time: 5 MINUTES   *cook time:* 15 MINUTES

Salt

8 ounces spaghetti (half a package)

1 tablespoon unsalted butter

4 cloves garlic, minced

½ cup heavy cream

Grated zest of 2 lemons

¼ cup fresh lemon juice

¼ cup freshly grated Parmesan cheese, plus more for serving

¼ cup chopped fresh basil

Freshly ground black pepper

Crushed red pepper flakes

Lemon slices, for garnish

IN a large pot of salted boiling water, cook the spaghetti to al dente according to the package directions.

MEANWHILE, in a large saucepan, melt the butter over medium heat. Add the garlic and sauté until fragrant, 2 to 3 minutes. Stir in the heavy cream, lemon zest, and lemon juice and simmer for 3 to 4 minutes.

DRAIN the pasta. Reduce the heat under the sauce to medium-low and fold in the cooked pasta, Parmesan, and basil. Cook for another 1 to 2 minutes to melt the cheese and wilt the basil.

SEASON with salt, black pepper, and pepper flakes to taste. Serve with more grated Parmesan and lemon slices.

Brussels Pasta

I fell in love with Brussels sprouts around the same time everyone else did a handful of years ago (I never knew there were so many flavorful ways to cook Brussels sprouts). My dad always hated Brussels sprouts, but now that he has had them in this dish, he's a fan.

This is one of my favorite spaghetti dishes to whip up. My kids will eat it and not even know they're eating a big green vegetable. (I love to try to sneak as many vegetables into my meals as possible.) Pour a glass of red wine and toast some French bread to serve with dipping oil, and you've got yourself a pretty fabulous meal.

MAKES 4 SERVINGS

prep time: 10 MINUTES   *cook time:* 15 MINUTES

Salt

10 ounces spaghetti

8 ounces pancetta, diced

4 tablespoons olive oil

2 cups thinly sliced Brussels sprouts

3 cloves garlic, minced

Juice of 1 lemon

1 teaspoon crushed red pepper flakes

Freshly ground black pepper

Grated Parmesan cheese, for serving

Freshly shaved Parmesan cheese, for serving

IN a large pot of salted boiling water, cook the spaghetti to al dente according to the package directions.

MEANWHILE, in a large skillet, cook the pancetta over medium heat just until it begins to crisp, about 2 to 3 minutes. Remove from the pan to paper towels to drain. Add 2 tablespoons of the oil to the pan with the pancetta grease. Add the Brussels sprouts and garlic and cook for about 10 minutes, turning the sprouts frequently, until they are tender but not soft. Reduce the heat to medium-low.

WHEN the pasta is done, drain and add to the Brussels sprouts. Fold in the pancetta, drizzle with the lemon juice, and heat over medium-low heat until heated through, about 2 minutes. Season with the pepper flakes and salt and black pepper to taste. Drizzle with the remaining 2 tablespoons oil. Add both grated and shaved Parmesan and give it a good toss to coat before serving.

Cold Pasta Salad

Pasta salad is a great dish to bring to picnics, church events, and family barbecues. It's something you can keep fresh and cold in your refrigerator until it's time to pop it out. You can make it the night before and it will be even better the next day after all the flavors have come together. Put it all in a beautiful bowl with wooden tongs and watch everyone come back for seconds.

MAKES 8 SERVINGS

prep time: **1 HOUR 5 MINUTES**   *cook time:* **15 MINUTES**

Salt

1 (16-ounce) package spaghetti

1 cup halved cherry tomatoes

1 cup diced cucumber

1 cup diced ham

1 green bell pepper, diced

½ small red onion, diced

½ (6-ounce) can black olives, thinly sliced

1 (8-ounce) bottle Italian salad dressing

1 cup grated Parmesan cheese

½ teaspoon paprika

Freshly ground black pepper

IN a large pot of salted boiling water, cook the spaghetti to al dente according to the package directions. Drain and rinse under cold water until room temperature.

IN a large bowl, combine the tomatoes, cucumber, ham, bell pepper, onion, olives, salad dressing, Parmesan, paprika, and black pepper to taste and toss well. Gently toss in the pasta. Refrigerate for at least 1 hour before serving.

Bucatini Calabrian Pasta

The spicy flair of southern Italian cuisine bursts through in this powerful tomato sauce with crushed Calabrian chiles and fresh basil. I went through a phase where I made this once a week for two months. I couldn't get enough licking my fingers taking in every last drop of sauce in my bowl. Serve with warm French bread and a fabulous red wine.

MAKES 4 SERVINGS

prep time: 5 MINUTES   _cook time:_ 15 MINUTES

Salt

12 ounces bucatini pasta

2 tablespoons olive oil

8 ounces thick-cut pancetta

3 cloves garlic, minced

1 (6-ounce) can tomato paste

1 to 2 tablespoons crushed Calabrian chiles packed in oil, to taste

1 teaspoon garlic powder

¼ teaspoon freshly ground black pepper

1 (14.5-ounce) can diced tomatoes

1 (15-ounce) can tomato sauce

½ teaspoon crushed red pepper flakes

5 fresh basil leaves, roughly chopped, plus more for serving

½ cup whole-milk ricotta cheese, for serving

IN a large pot of salted boiling water, cook the bucatini to al dente according to the package directions. Drain.

MEANWHILE, in a large deep skillet, heat the oil over medium heat. Add the pancetta and garlic and sauté until the pancetta begins to crisp, about 5 minutes.

WHISK in the tomato paste and Calabrian chiles and season with the garlic powder, black pepper, and 1 teaspoon salt. Continue to cook and stir for 2 to 3 minutes, or until the mixture begins to simmer.

POUR off a little of the liquid from the diced tomatoes, then add to the pan. Stir in the tomato sauce and bring to a simmer. Reduce the heat to low and continue to cook for 5 to 7 minutes to cook off some of the moisture.

WHEN the pasta is done and the sauce has cooked together, add the pepper flakes and basil. Fold in the drained pasta with tongs and toss to coat in the sauce, continuing to cook over low heat for 1 to 2 more minutes.

PLATE and serve with a basil leaf and a dollop of ricotta.

Bolognese Sauce

Bolognese is so much more than just a meat sauce. It is a whole mood. Between the pancetta and vegetables that set the tone, to the olive oil and ground veal and tomato paste, to the friendly splash of white wine, this is a recipe I take personal pride in.

I make both my Seafood Gumbo (page 171) and this Bolognese with no directions and just know they will come out amazing every time. We have this Bolognese weekly, and I know after you make it in your kitchen it will become a weekly go-to for your home, too.

MAKES 2½ HEAPING CUPS

prep time: 10 MINUTES   *cook time:* 1 HOUR

3 tablespoons olive oil
½ pound ground veal
½ pound ground pork
½ pound ground beef
2 ounces pancetta, finely chopped
3 cloves garlic, minced
1 cup chopped carrots
1 medium onion, chopped
1 stalk celery, chopped
½ cup white wine
1 (6-ounce) can tomato paste
1 (15-ounce) can tomato sauce
1 cup half-and-half

IN a large skillet, heat the oil over medium heat. Brown the meats, about 6 to 8 minutes, breaking them up into large clumps as you go. Transfer the browned meat to a large bowl and discard any drippings from the pan.

IN the same pan, fry the pancetta until crisp, 5 to 7 minutes. Add the garlic, carrots, onion, and celery and cook over medium heat, stirring occasionally, until the vegetables begin to soften, about 5 minutes.

RETURN the browned meat to the pan and pour in the wine. Simmer and let the wine reduce by half, then stir in the tomato paste, tomato sauce, and half-and-half. Partially cover the pan and continue to slow-cook for about 45 minutes, stirring occasionally, until ready to serve.

tip

To serve over pasta, cook 1 (1-pound) box tagliatelle in a large pot of salted boiling water according to the package directions. Drain and rinse. Serve the meat sauce over the pasta and garnish with 1 tablespoon chopped parsley.

Ground Chicken Lasagna

I love the traditional ground beef lasagna, but I wanted to create a different version to switch it up once in a while. I've told y'all how I like to sneak vegetables in as many things as I can, so I know my babies are getting their daily greens. In this recipe I managed to sneak in carrots, mushrooms, and spinach, which they will never know because it's so flavorful and delicious with every cheesy bite.

MAKES 10 TO 12 SERVINGS

prep time: 20 MINUTES   *cook time:* 1 HOUR

Salt

9 lasagna noodles

3 tablespoons olive oil

1 medium onion, chopped

1 cup diced carrots

1 head garlic (9 to 10 cloves), minced

1 (4-ounce) can mushrooms, drained

1 tablespoon tomato paste

Freshly ground black pepper

Garlic powder

1 pound lean ground chicken

5 cups spinach leaves

1 (24-ounce) jar marinara sauce

1 (15-ounce) container ricotta cheese

1 (8-ounce) bag shredded mozzarella cheese

Basil

IN a large pot of salted boiling water, cook the lasagna noodles according to the package directions. Drain and spread out on a baking sheet.

IN a large skillet, heat 2 tablespoons of the oil over medium heat. Add the onion and carrots and sauté until tender, about 3 minutes. Add the garlic and cook for about 2 minutes, until fragrant. Add the mushrooms, tomato paste, pepper, garlic powder, and chicken and cook until the meat begins to brown, about 6 minutes. Add the spinach a handful at a time and stir until it wilts, about 1 minute. Remove from the heat.

PREHEAT the oven to 400°F. Grease a 9 × 13-inch baking dish with the remaining 1 tablespoon olive oil.

LAYER the bottom of the dish with 3 cooked lasagna noodles. Top it with half of the chicken mixture, followed by about 1 cup of marinara sauce, a third of the ricotta, and ⅔ cup of the mozzarella. Repeat this for the second layer of lasagna noodles, remaining chicken mixture, 1 cup marinara sauce, a third of the ricotta, and ⅔ cup mozzarella. Top with the final layer of lasagna noodles, cover with the remaining 1 cup of marinara sauce, and top with the remaining ricotta and mozzarella. (If not baking right away, cover and refrigerate the lasagna until the next day.)

TRANSFER the lasagna to the oven and bake, 30 to 40 minutes. The lasagna is ready when a toothpick sinks into the center, showing that the noodles are tender. Let the lasagna cool down 15 to 20 minutes before serving.

I'm a Sides Chick

I'm a sides chick . . . get it? Ask any of my friends, family, or business associates. Anytime we go out to eat we order six different sides. I remember the first few times Eric and I went out on dates and his eyes widened at the number of sides I ordered! He had met his match, someone who loved food as much as he did.

Of course, I don't eat all of it, but I just like to take a little taste of everything. I love variety and I love different flavors. I never skip sides. I love them so much I have a whole list of sides to share with you from my kitchen to yours. Some of these sides are recipes I fell in love with at restaurants or at other people's homes and was inspired to come up with my own versions.

Cauliflower Potato Salad

When I was pregnant with Vivianne, I experienced the worst morning sickness out of any of my pregnancies. I was bedridden for the first five months and could keep down only a few things. It was awful, because I was so nauseous all the time but also so hungry. The only way to make my nausea subside was to keep my belly full. My sense of smell was so heightened, and pretty much every smell—including metal for crying out loud!—made me want to puke for that first four months. Luckily my amazing sister was living with us to help out after I got pregnant. (Eric was at football practice all day.) One day she suggested a few ideas that didn't seem so bad. We figured out I could keep down potato salad, fruit salad, and cinnamon rolls! I am so grateful to have had my amazing sister on hand to make this potato salad on demand whenever her nauseous pregnant sister was asking for it.

This potato salad is even better when you're not having morning sickness. It was my mama's recipe, but I decided to add a twist and make it my own by adding my lovely cauliflower! In our family we like to serve potato salad at room temperature.

MAKES 6 SERVINGS

prep time: 10 MINUTES   *cook time:* 10 MINUTES

3 pounds potatoes (russet or red)

Salt

½ head cauliflower, cut into large pieces

3 hard-boiled eggs (see Tip), sliced

¼ small Vidalia onion, slivered

¾ cup mayonnaise (I prefer Blue Plate)

2 tablespoons dill relish, or to taste

1 tablespoon yellow mustard

Freshly ground black pepper

Paprika

Tony Chachere's Creole Seasoning

PEEL and quarter the potatoes, place in a medium pot, cover with water, and add a pinch of salt. Bring to a boil over medium-high heat, and cook the potatoes for 6 to 8 minutes. Add the cauliflower and cook for 1 to 3 more minutes. Drain and place in a large bowl to cool.

ADD the eggs, onion, mayo, relish, mustard, and black pepper, paprika, and Tony's seasoning to taste. With a large spoon, carefully fold together, taking care not to mash the potatoes too much.

SERVE immediately at room temperature, not too hot, not too cold—think Goldilocks and the Three Bears, just right!

tip

I boil the eggs in the same pot as the potatoes.

Fruit Salad

This is a family recipe that my mom has been making for years. It's like candy in a bowl. This is another one of those dishes that I craved when I was pregnant with Vivi. You will find me saying this quite a lot in this cookbook because I ate like nobody's business when I was pregnant with my first, ha! But I wanted this salad over and over again, so on top of my sister making me potato salad frequently, she also made me our family fruit salad. The cream with the marshmallows and the bits of mandarin oranges and grapes will burst into your mouth with every bite. Yummy!

MAKES 6 SERVINGS

prep time: 15 MINUTES

1 pint cold heavy cream

2 tablespoons sugar

1 teaspoon pure vanilla extract

2 large apples, chopped (peeled or unpeeled, a matter of taste)

1 (15-ounce) can water-packed mandarin oranges, drained

1 cup sliced strawberries

1 (20-ounce) can pineapple chunks packed in juice, well drained

3 cups green seedless grapes (cotton candy grapes if you can find them), halved

2 firm-ripe bananas, sliced

1 (4-ounce) jar maraschino cherries, halved and drained

2 cups mini marshmallows

IN a medium bowl, with an electric mixer or whisk, beat the cream with the sugar and vanilla to firm peaks, about 7 minutes.

IN a large bowl, combine the apples, oranges, strawberries, pineapple, grapes, bananas, and maraschinos and toss to combine. Gently fold in the marshmallows and whipped cream.

SERVE immediately.

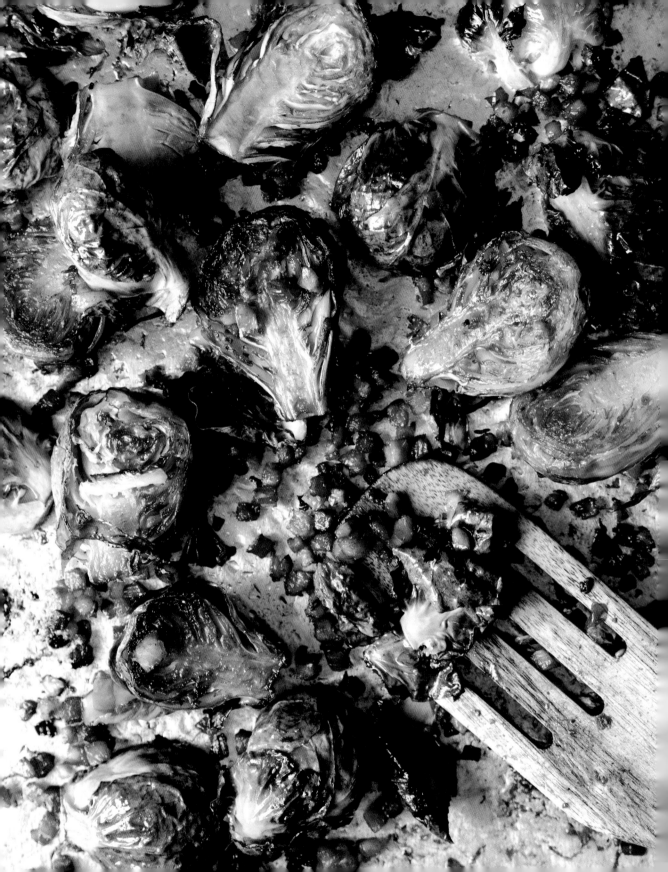

Brussels Sprouts and Pancetta

This dish is like candied vegetables with meat. Anytime I go out to eat and Brussels sprouts are on the menu, you better believe I'm ordering them. My best friend, Jessica, was the first to introduce me to Brussels sprouts when she would order them on our girl dates, and she got me hooked. This is one of my favorite Brussels recipes, and I cook it frequently.

MAKES 4 TO 6 SERVINGS

prep time: 10 MINUTES   *cook time:* 30 MINUTES

1½ pounds Brussels sprouts, trimmed and halved

3 cloves garlic, minced

¼ cup olive oil

¼ cup balsamic vinegar

4 ounces pancetta, cut into ½-inch dice (see Tip)

Salt and freshly ground black pepper

tip

I buy pre-diced pancetta. Very convenient.

PREHEAT the oven to 400°F. Line a sheet pan with foil or parchment paper.

IN a large bowl, toss together the Brussels sprouts, garlic, 2 tablespoons of the oil, and the vinegar.

SPREAD the Brussels sprouts, along with any leaves that may have fallen off, and the pancetta in a single layer on the prepared baking sheet. Drizzle with the remaining 2 tablespoons oil, sprinkle with 1 teaspoon salt and ¼ teaspoon pepper, and toss to coat.

ROAST the Brussels sprouts until they're tender and nicely browned and the pancetta is cooked, 20 to 30 minutes, tossing once at the 20-minute mark.

REMOVE from the oven. Taste and adjust the seasoning with salt and pepper. Serve hot.

Green Beans with Almonds and Sea Salt

At the age of two I began snapping beans fresh from the garden at Maw Maw's house. I love me some green beans and cook with them frequently in many different dishes. This recipe is great alongside roasted chicken and mashed potatoes. It's also a perfect side at Thanksgiving or Christmas dinner.

MAKES 4 SERVINGS

prep time: 10 MINUTES   *cook time:* 20 MINUTES

1 tablespoon olive oil

½ cup chopped onion

2 cloves garlic, minced

1 pound green beans, trimmed

Sea salt and freshly ground
  black pepper

2 tablespoons slivered
  almonds, toasted

IN a large skillet, heat the oil over medium-low heat. Add the onions and slow-cook for about 10 minutes, stirring occasionally, until tender and beginning to caramelize. Add the garlic and continue to cook for 3 minutes.

INCREASE the heat to medium and add the green beans. Season with salt and pepper to taste. Cover and cook, tossing frequently to make sure they cook evenly, until tender, 7 to 10 minutes.

GARNISH with the slivered almonds and serve.

Bacon-Wrapped Asparagus

When I was a kid, there were only two kinds of green vegetables you could get me to eat: green beans and asparagus. Green beans make sense, I think, but asparagus is a weird one to like at the age of six, right? Well, my love for asparagus just continues to grow as I come up with new ways to use the magical vegetable. I grew up eating bacon-wrapped green beans, so I decided to not leave out my asparagus and let them join in on the bacon fun, too.

This is a pretty easy recipe and can be done quickly if ya need to throw an appetizer together. I love using maple syrup to add that sweetness to the bacon. Enjoy this one. OK, my mouth is watering now.

MAKES 8 SERVINGS

prep time: 5 MINUTES   *cook time:* 20 MINUTES

1½ pounds asparagus, tough ends trimmed

2 tablespoons olive oil

Salt and freshly ground black pepper

4 slices thick-cut bacon, halved lengthwise

½ cup balsamic vinegar

¼ cup maple syrup

PREHEAT the oven to 425°F. Line a baking sheet with parchment paper.

ARRANGE the asparagus on the prepared baking sheet, drizzle with the oil, and season with salt and pepper to taste. Gently turn the asparagus with tongs to coat.

DIVIDE the asparagus into 8 bunches of 3 to 5 spears each. Wrap each with a strip of bacon.

LAY the bacon bunches seam side down and roast until the bacon has browned and the asparagus is tender, about 20 minutes. Turn the oven to broil for the last few minutes of cooking, until the asparagus bundles are crispy. Watch this, though, because I've burned this a few times in my day.

MEANWHILE, in a small saucepan over medium-high heat, cook the vinegar and maple syrup to a glaze, stirring occasionally, 5 to 10 minutes. Let the glaze cool to thicken up.

DRIZZLE the glaze over the asparagus bunches before serving.

Sweet Potato Pecan Bake

Every Thanksgiving I get the most excited about this dish, even more than the turkey. I could eat an entire pan of this by myself. The combo of pecans, butter, and brown sugar with marshmallows makes my mouth melt as I'm typing this right now. I'm not trying to limit this dish to just Thanksgiving—it's great for any time of year ya want—but it's most famous for being one of the sides on Thanksgiving, so I highly recommend this fabulous sweet potato dish for your next Turkey Day meal.

MAKES 14 TO 16 SERVINGS

prep time: 15 MINUTES   *cook time:* 40 MINUTES

Cooking spray, for the baking dish

2½ pounds sweet potatoes, peeled and halved

1 cup packed light brown sugar

8 tablespoons (1 stick) unsalted butter, at room temperature

1½ teaspoons salt

1 teaspoon pure vanilla extract

½ cup finely chopped pecans

2 cups miniature marshmallows

PREHEAT the oven to 375°F. Coat a glass or ceramic 3-quart baking dish with cooking spray.

IN a large pot of boiling water over medium-high heat, cook the sweet potatoes until tender, about 15 minutes. Drain and let cool.

IN a large bowl, combine the cooled sweet potatoes, brown sugar, butter, salt, and vanilla and mash until smooth.

STIR in ¼ cup of the pecans, then scoop into the prepared baking dish. Top with the remaining ¼ cup pecans and the mini marshmallows.

BAKE until golden, about 25 minutes. Remove from the oven and serve.

Cilantro-Lime Rice

This is so easy and quick and I always make it for taco night with a side of black beans! A secret is I hate making rice, so I get the microwavable boxed rice from Trader Joe's or Whole Foods and I've never told anyone until now—ha! Why go through all that darn trouble when it tastes just the same?

MAKES 4 TO 6 SERVINGS

prep time: 5 MINUTES   *cook time:* 8 MINUTES

2 (10-ounce) bags frozen rice, cooked according to package directions (I use Trader Joe's frozen jasmine rice)

1 tablespoon avocado oil

Juice of 1 lime

3 tablespoons finely chopped fresh cilantro

½ teaspoon sea salt

Freshly ground black pepper

FLUFF the cooked rice with a fork, then fold in the avocado oil, lime juice, and chopped cilantro. Season with the sea salt and pepper to taste before serving.

Cheese, Sauce, and Bread, Oh My!

Pizza pizza pizza! Just like Selena Quintanilla told us she could eat an entire medium pizza by herself, I would have to say the same for myself! I love pizza so much and am always down to have it. I'm pretty picky about pizza and am one of those crazy people who will search every single Yelp review and picture so that I can find the absolute best pizza there is before committing to ordering it or heading to the restaurant. I have a unique skill (my mom has it, too) where I can tell by just looking at a picture if the food is going to be good. I do this with every new restaurant I go to.

Anyway, back to the pizza . . . My favorite kind of pizza is either deep-dish or coal fire brick oven style. One of our good friends and old neighbors has a pizza oven and it got so addicting that I was practically inviting myself over every chance I got when I smelled the oven firing up! I love homemade pizza more than takeout or delivery, so lucky for me Eric got me a pizza oven for Christmas, and now I'm obsessed with it. You don't need a pizza oven to make these at all. A regular oven will be just fine, so here are a handful of my favorite pizza recipes. Lots of variety from simple to decadent for anyone's taste buds.

Honey, Arugula, and Pepperoni Naan Pizza

My honey, arugula, and pepperoni pizza is my favorite of them all. What really makes this pizza special is that drizzle of honey that tops it off. I invite friends over for pizza night quite frequently, and this is a hit every time.

People are always asking me for the recipe, and when I tell them how simple it is, they don't believe me: They think I'm leaving out some sort of secret ingredient. I'm giving you all the secrets right here, and I promise you it lies in that honey drizzle at the very end.

You can use a fresh dough if you have the time to make it, but if not, go for the naan bread— you can find it at any grocery store and it is the absolute perfect pizza crust.

MAKES 2 TO 4 SERVINGS

prep time: 10 MINUTES   *cook time:* 10 MINUTES

2 naan breads

2 tablespoons olive oil

¼ cup pizza sauce

¼ teaspoon garlic powder

Salt and freshly ground black pepper

2 cups shredded 4-cheese pizza blend (I use Trader Joe's Quattro Formaggio)

8 to 12 slices pepperoni, or more to taste

1 cup baby arugula

Grated Parmesan cheese, for serving

1 tablespoon fresh lemon juice

Honey, for drizzling

PREHEAT the oven to 425°F.

PLACE the naan on a baking sheet. Brush the naans with the oil and spoon on the pizza sauce. Season with the garlic powder and salt and pepper to taste. Add a generous handful or two of shredded cheese and layer on the pepperoni.

TRANSFER to the oven and bake until the cheese is melted and bubbling, 5 to 7 minutes. (You could also cook these on a grill or in a wood-fire pizza oven!)

REMOVE from the oven and top each pizza with a handful of arugula, grated Parmesan, a squeeze of lemon juice, and a drizzle of honey.

Quattro Formaggi Naan Pizza

This pizza is perfect for your little ones. Now don't let me fool you, this is the perfect pizza for anyone, but if your little ones are not too crazy about all the sauces and honey, this is a fancy version of cheese pizza: Quattro formaggi means "four cheeses." Trader Joe's sells an excellent four-cheese blend called Quattro Formaggio that I highly recommend using for this pizza.

If you want to get a little fancy with it, you can sprinkle some basil on top when this baby comes out of the oven.

MAKES 2 TO 4 SERVINGS

prep time: 5 MINUTES　　*cook time:* 7 MINUTES

2 naan breads

1 tablespoon olive oil

¼ teaspoon garlic powder

Salt and freshly ground black pepper

2 cups Trader Joe's Quattro Formaggio or other 4-cheese Italian blend

PREHEAT the oven to 425°F.

PLACE the naans on a baking sheet. Brush the naans with the oil and season with the garlic powder and salt and pepper to taste. Divide the shredded cheese over the naans and spread evenly.

TRANSFER to the oven and bake until the cheese is melted and bubbling, 5 to 7 minutes. Simple and fabulous.

Bolognese Pizza

Anytime I make my delicious Bolognese sauce for pasta, I always plan to make pizzas the next day. It started when our friends, who have a pizza oven in their kitchen, invited us all over for a pizza party. One of the other guests happened to be a chef. He brought a Bolognese sauce he had made a few days prior and spread it all over fresh dough and put it in the oven. One bite, and I was hooked.

This is a great way to not let leftover Bolognese go to waste. And when my sister hears I'm making it she comes a-runnin'!

MAKES 8 SERVINGS

prep time: 15 MINUTES   *cook time:* 20 MINUTES

1 tablespoon olive oil, plus more (optional) for the pan

1 pound refrigerated pizza dough (I use Publix brand)

2 cups shredded 4-cheese pizza blend (I use Trader Joe's Quattro Formaggio)

1 cup Bolognese Sauce (page 91), or store-bought Bolognese

Salt and freshly ground black pepper

Crushed red pepper flakes

PREHEAT the oven to 400°F.

TURN the dough out onto a nonstick or lightly greased pizza pan and form into a round.

BRUSH the dough with the oil and top with most of the cheese, all the Bolognese sauce, and another sprinkling of cheese.

TRANSFER to the oven and bake until the crust is browned and the cheese is melted, about 18 minutes (depending on the thickness of the dough). Season with salt, black pepper, and pepper flakes to taste.

BBQ Chicken Pizza

For as long as I can remember, my parents have been putting chicken on their pizza, and when I was younger, I thought it was so unique. As an adult, I realize it's pretty common, but I still think it's a cool way to switch it up from your typical pepperoni.

My husband in particular loves it because he goes through phases where he doesn't want a ton of red meat or beef and wants to stick to fish and chicken, so this is the perfect way to enjoy homemade pizza and still get some meat. I especially love the added BBQ sauce and the red onion crunch. It makes it feel like a pizza party in my mouth.

I highly recommend the Sriracha BBQ sauce from Trader Joe's for anything BBQ! It has just enough kick to add that little bit of flare.

MAKES 8 SERVINGS

prep time: 15 MINUTES   *cook time:* 20 MINUTES

1 tablespoon olive oil, plus more (optional) for the pan

2 cups shredded cooked chicken breast

½ cup barbecue sauce

1 pound refrigerated pizza dough (I use Publix brand)

1 cup pizza sauce (see Tip)

2 cups shredded 4-cheese pizza blend (I use Trader Joe's Quattro Formaggio)

¼ teaspoon garlic powder

Salt and freshly ground black pepper

½ cup thinly sliced red onion

PREHEAT the oven to 400°F.

IN a medium bowl, toss together the shredded chicken and barbecue sauce and set aside.

TURN the dough out onto a nonstick or lightly greased pizza pan and form it into a round.

BRUSH the dough with the oil and top with the pizza sauce and shredded cheese. Season with the garlic powder and salt and pepper to taste. Layer on the chicken mixture and red onion.

TRANSFER to the oven and bake until the crust is browned and the cheese is melted, about 18 minutes (depending on the thickness of the dough).

tip

If you don't have pizza sauce, you can use marinara sauce seasoned with salt, pepper, garlic powder, and Italian seasoning.

I'm All About That....
Meat

I'm all about my meat.

Ah, meat . . . I just love it. I really do.

I'm one of those gals that needs meat with every single meal or it just doesn't feel like a meal. It's not because I'm stubborn or ignorant, it's just because that's how my body feels. I don't feel right when I don't have my meat. I've watched all the documentaries you can think of and listened to lots of people share their educated opinions—and I truly respect them—but meatless just doesn't work for me. I tried to go vegan for a week once, and I'll be honest: it wasn't bad, but it just wasn't for me.

I love bacon with everything, I love steak, I love my Bolognese, and I love my pepperoni.

I distinctly remember being very pregnant and headed to a football game on a private plane with some fellow football wives who were all vegan. I tried so hard to enjoy the vegan cheese and bean burritos they so kindly shared and passed around, but by the time I got to the football stadium I felt like I was gonna pass out and had to order a cheeseburger immediately.

So you get it, OK, I love meat. Here are some of my favorite meaty recipes.

Flank Steak and Corn Salad

This is one of those meals that makes Eric and me giddy, and I can't really put my finger on it. I think maybe it's the big ol' fiesta with all of our favorite things on one plate. I'll go ahead and list 'em off: Steak, check. Corn, check. Cheese, check. Arugula, tomatoes, avocado . . . I mean ya just can't go wrong.

Eric and I love to make this one together. I'll do the salad as he throws the steak on the grill. We will enjoy this in the middle of hot summers and make my homemade Skinny Margs (page 243) and sit outside by the pool talking about our feelings and of course the delicious flavorful meat on our plates.

MAKES 6 TO 8 SERVINGS

prep time: 15 MINUTES   *cook time:* 15 MINUTES

FOR THE CHARRED CORN

2 tablespoons olive oil

1 (10-ounce) bag frozen white corn kernels

Salt and freshly ground black pepper

FOR THE STEAK

1 tablespoon smoked paprika

2 tablespoons light brown sugar

1 tablespoon salt

1 tablespoon freshly ground black pepper

2 teaspoons chili powder

2 teaspoons ground cumin

2 teaspoons garlic powder

2 teaspoons onion powder

2 pounds flank steak

Avocado oil or olive oil, for greasing

FOR THE SALAD

1 (5-ounce) package baby arugula

1 avocado, chopped

char the corn: In a large skillet, heat the oil over medium heat. Add the frozen corn and season with salt and pepper to taste. Cook, stirring frequently, until the corn begins to char, about 5 minutes. Remove from the heat.

prepare the steak: In a small bowl, combine the paprika, brown sugar, salt, pepper, chili powder, cumin, garlic powder, and onion powder and mix well. Rub the seasonings on both sides of the steak.

HEAT a large skillet or grill pan over medium-high heat and drizzle in some oil. Add the seasoned flank steak and cook until it begins to char slightly, about 3 minutes on each side. A meat thermometer inserted into the thickest part of the steak should read 130°F. Remove from the pan and let rest for at least 15 minutes to keep the juices from running.

½ red onion, chopped

1 cup cherry tomatoes, halved

½ cup fresh lime juice (4 or 5 limes)

2 tablespoons olive oil

1 tablespoon honey

Salt and freshly ground black pepper

Shredded Cheddar cheese, for serving

assemble the salad: In a large bowl, layer the arugula, charred corn, avocado, onion, tomatoes, lime juice, oil, honey, and salt and pepper to taste and toss to combine.

CUT the meat into ½-inch slices, top with the corn salad and shredded cheese, and serve.

Eric's Brazilian Steak and Black Beans

This is one of the few meals I've ever seen Eric make, and the story behind it is kind of funny. My first trip to visit Eric in Denver was a learning experience for me. If you've ever seen the episode of Friends *where "Joey doesn't share food"—well, I learned quickly that Eric doesn't share food either.*

This was day four of my trip and we were still getting to know each other, and let's just say I was starving. At the time, he was living with Demaryius, another football player, and every morning that I was there, they went to work and ate lunch at the facility. I was left behind with no food and no vehicle. I would wait for Eric to come back so we could head to dinner—and then I would eat all I could.

On one of the days, Eric came back to the house for lunch and went into the kitchen to cook up this recipe. I patiently waited for my lunch. It smelled so good as the steak sizzled. And then I realized that he had put the entire thing on his plate, which he carried with him to the couch. I was perplexed and so hungry. I sat down next to him and explained that I was starving and that it was time to share food. It was as if he had no idea, being a bachelor for so long. To this day I can still make him laugh about it.

The recipe he made was simpler than the one laid out below. But the steak and beans and white rice were so delicious that I decided to create our own version of it, and every time I make it, I give him that little smirk and pretend that I'm not going to share it with him.

MAKES 2 SERVINGS

prep time: 2 HOURS   *cook time:* 10 MINUTES

FOR THE STEAK

2 tablespoons unsalted butter, melted

1 tablespoon Worcestershire sauce

2 teaspoons ground cumin

½ teaspoon garlic powder

Salt and freshly ground black pepper

1 pound rib eye steak

1 tablespoon olive oil

prepare the steak: In a small bowl, whisk together the melted butter, Worcestershire sauce, cumin, garlic powder, and salt and pepper to taste. Place the steak in a plastic bag or glass bowl and cover with the mixture. Let marinate for 2 hours in the refrigerator.

HEAT a large heavy skillet or grill pan over high heat for 1 minute. Add the oil and seasoned steak and cook over medium to medium-high heat, 3 to 4 minutes on each side, depending on the thickness of the rib eye, for medium-rare. Remove from the heat and let rest for 15 minutes.

FOR THE BEANS

1 tablespoon olive oil

½ cup diced yellow onion

2 cloves garlic, minced

1 (15.5-ounce) can black beans, rinsed and drained

½ teaspoon garlic powder

Salt and freshly ground black pepper

FOR SERVING

Cooked white rice

½ cup diced Roma (plum) tomatoes

Flat-leaf parsley, for garnish

meanwhile, make the beans: In a medium saucepan, heat the oil over medium heat. Add the onion and garlic and cook until fragrant, about 3 minutes. Stir in the black beans, garlic powder, and salt and pepper to taste. Keep warm over low heat until ready to serve.

to serve: Slice the steak across the grain and serve with white rice, diced tomatoes, and seasoned black beans. Garnish with parsley.

Barbacoa Bowls

You will fall in love with this dish of slow-cooked chuck roast with rice, pickled red onions, and vegetables. This is a great one to make when having friends and family over.

I like to put the sides in little bowls with serving spoons for guests to help themselves to as much as they want. When guests can put together their own bowls, they feel more a part of the meal.

MAKES 8 SERVINGS

prep time: 15 MINUTES   *cook time:* 6 TO 8 HOURS

FOR THE BARBACOA BEEF

4 pounds chuck roast

1 teaspoon kosher salt

1 teaspoon freshly ground black pepper

1 tablespoon olive oil

1 cup beef broth

½ cup apple cider vinegar

Juice of 3 limes

6 garlic cloves, peeled

4 canned chipotle peppers in adobo sauce (see Tip)

4 teaspoons ground cumin

2 teaspoons dried oregano

½ teaspoon ground cloves

5 bay leaves

FOR THE BOWLS

Shredded or chopped lettuce

Whole kernel yellow corn

Black beans, at room temperature or chilled

Cooked white rice

Pickled Red Onions (recipe follows)

Shredded Mexican cheese blend (optional)

Chopped fresh cilantro

make the barbacoa beef: Set a skillet over medium-high heat. Season the roast with the salt and pepper and drizzle on the oil. Add to the hot skillet and sear each side, 1 to 2 minutes per side.

IN a blender, combine the broth, vinegar, lime juice, garlic, chipotles, cumin, oregano, and ground cloves and puree. Place the seared roast in a slow cooker, pour in the sauce, and add the bay leaves. Cover and cook on high for 6 to 8 hours.

ONCE the roast is nice and tender, remove the bay leaves and shred the beef with two forks.

build the bowls: Line a salad bowl with lettuce. Layer on the shredded barbacoa beef, corn, beans, and rice. Top with pickled red onions, cheese (if using), and cilantro before serving.

tip

If you are sensitive to spicy food, reduce the chipotles to 1 or 2. This dish has some heat!

Pickled Red Onions

MAKES 4 SERVINGS

1 medium red onion, thinly
  sliced

¾ cup apple cider vinegar

1 tablespoon sugar

1 teaspoon salt

PLACE the onion in a glass container or jar. Combine the
vinegar, sugar, and salt and pour the mixture over the
onions. Let sit for at least 30 minutes or up to 2 hours.
Drain before using.

Juicy Cheeseburgers

This is the all-American girl side of me. Let me tell you I can tear up a good juicy cheeseburger. I came up with this particular cheeseburger recipe one Fourth of July when we were down in Florida on vacation. I saw a gorgeous picture of a juicy cheeseburger on Instagram and immediately raced up to our local grocery store to create my own version. This is one of the best cheeseburgers I've ever had in my life—it truly is juicy!

MAKES 6 SERVINGS

prep time: 15 MINUTES   *cook time:* 15 MINUTES

FOR MY FANCY SAUCE

½ cup Hellmann's mayonnaise

1 tablespoon Dijon mustard

2 teaspoons ketchup

¼ teaspoon dried dill

Pinch of cayenne pepper

FOR THE BURGERS

1½ pounds 80/20 ground beef

6 King's Hawaiian buns, split (see Tip)

4 tablespoons unsalted butter, melted

1 tablespoon garlic powder

½ teaspoon Tony Chachere's Creole Seasoning

Salt and freshly ground black pepper

6 slices Cheddar cheese

6 leaves green leaf lettuce

12 slices tomato (¼ inch thick)

tip

Don't skimp on the bun! I highly recommend getting the King's Hawaiian hamburger buns.

make my fancy sauce: In a small bowl, stir together the mayo, mustard, ketchup, dill, and cayenne until smooth. Set aside.

make the burgers: Form the beef into 6 patties 1 inch thick.

HEAT a cast-iron skillet or grill pan over medium-low heat.

BRUSH the split rolls with melted butter, and place them cut side down on the skillet until toasted, 2 to 3 minutes. Transfer to a plate while you grill the burgers.

INCREASE the heat to medium and let the pan get hot. Season both sides of each beef patty with the garlic powder, Tony's seasoning, and salt and black pepper to taste.

PLACE the burger patties in the pan and flatten each slightly with a wide spatula. Cook the patties until the juices are bubbling out and the underside is beginning to brown, 3 to 4 minutes. Flip and top each patty with a slice of cheddar. Continue to grill until medium, 3 to 4 minutes.

BUILD the burgers with a patty on each bottom bun, followed by a lettuce leaf and 2 tomato slices. Spread the fancy sauce on the top bun to finish it off before serving.

Dirty Rice and Beans

This is the type of dish where you basically just throw all sorts of things together into one pot. This is for you mamas during times when you have run out of things and don't have time to go to the grocery store and need to pull something together out of thin air. If you follow my directions in the beginning of the book and always have canned mushrooms, packaged sausage, and canned beans, you can pull off anything. I'm all about making life easier for hardworkin' mamas who are short on time. Plus, this is a great way to avoid ordering takeout or heating up something up in the microwave. It's homemade and easy, and I like it!

This gets the "quick feeds" stamp of approval for the mom-on-the-go.

MAKES 4 SERVINGS

prep time: 10 MINUTES   *cook time:* 20 MINUTES

1 tablespoon olive oil

½ red bell pepper, diced

½ green bell pepper, diced

½ cup sliced white mushrooms

½ cup diced red onion

1 (14-ounce) package kielbasa, sliced ¼ inch thick

1 (15.5-ounce) can pinto beans, rinsed and drained

4 cups cooked instant brown rice, or frozen brown rice

1 tablespoon Italian seasoning

Salt and freshly ground black pepper

IN a large skillet, heat the oil over medium heat. Add the peppers, mushrooms, and onion and cook until the peppers and onion are soft, about 5 minutes. Add the sausage and let that fry until it just starts to brown, about 5 minutes. Stir in the pinto beans and brown rice and cook just until everything is heated through, 6 to 10 minutes. Season with the Italian seasoning and salt and black pepper to taste before serving.

10-Can Chili

A girlfriend of mine had this delicious chili cooking on her stove on Halloween night while we took the babies trick-or-treating in the neighborhood. When we came back, we each had a bowl and I fell in love with the meaty chili and bites of corn and green beans. I'm a huge chili lover and always have been, so I'm constantly looking for all kinds of variations to create!

This is a good one. You can use ground beef, ground chicken, or ground turkey. All taste amazing!

MAKES 6 SERVINGS

prep time: 15 MINUTES   *cook time:* 20 MINUTES

2 tablespoons olive oil

2 cloves garlic, chopped

3 carrots, chopped

1 medium yellow onion, chopped

1 pound ground beef

1 (10-ounce) can Ro-tel diced tomatoes and green chilies

3 (15.5-ounce) cans kidney beans, rinsed and drained

2 (15.25-ounce) cans white corn

1 (15-ounce) can vegetarian chili

1 (15-ounce) can tomato sauce

2 (14.5-ounce) cans cut green beans

2 tablespoons chili powder

1 tablespoon garlic powder

1 teaspoon ground cumin

Tony Chachere's Creole Seasoning

Salt and freshly ground black pepper

Shredded Cheddar cheese, for serving

Chopped fresh cilantro, for garnish

Tortilla chips, for serving

IN a large pot, heat the oil over medium heat. Add the garlic and sauté until fragrant, about 2 to 3 minutes. Add the carrots and onion and when they start to soften, after about 5 minutes, add the beef and brown for about 7 minutes, breaking it up with a wooden spatula or spoon. Drain the fat from the meat and discard the drippings.

STIR in the tomatoes with green chilies, kidney beans, corn, vegetarian chili, tomato sauce, and green beans and cook for 5 minutes. Stir in the chili powder, garlic powder, cumin, and Tony's seasoning and salt and pepper to taste. Cover, reduce the heat to low, and simmer until you are ready to eat.

TOP with Cheddar, garnish with cilantro, and serve with tortilla chips.

Beef and Bean Enchiladas

If you haven't noticed yet, I really love beans and I really love beef, which I'm sure y'all find really sexy (LOL). I just think you can make so many delicious meals with beef and beans! One being beef and bean enchiladas.

I cook plenty of dishes that leave leftovers for the next day, which is always great for lunch for the kids, but when we have beef and bean enchiladas there ain't nothing left by the end of the night.

There are so many different ways to make enchiladas, as y'all know (if you got my first book it had a recipe for chicken enchiladas), but I wanted to share these enchiladas because I think the added corn and variety of beans that I use is unique. Y'all will not regret making this one. "Beans beans the magical fruit, add your beef and cheese to suit!"

MAKES 10 SERVINGS

1 pound ground beef

1¼ cups enchilada sauce (see Tip)

1 cup rinsed and drained canned black beans

1 cup rinsed and drained canned pinto beans

1 (12-ounce) bag frozen white corn kernels

3 tablespoons olive oil or vegetable oil

10 (10-inch) flour tortillas

2 cups shredded Monterey Jack or Cheddar cheese

3 tablespoons finely chopped cilantro, for garnish

Chopped scallions, for garnish

Sour cream, for serving

tip

If you happen to have my first book, Just Jessie, check out my homemade enchilada sauce.

prep time: 10 MINUTES *cook time:* 40 MINUTES

IN a large skillet, brown the beef over medium-high heat, about 7 minutes. Drain off the fat from the pan. Stir ¼ cup of the enchilada sauce into the meat mixture. Add the black beans, pinto beans, and corn. Reduce the heat to medium and simmer for 1 to 2 minutes.

PREHEAT the oven to 350°F.

SPREAD ½ cup of the enchilada sauce onto the bottom of a 9 × 13-inch glass baking dish.

IN a medium skillet, heat the oil over medium heat. Lightly fry each tortilla for 30 seconds on one side, just to warm it and make it more pliable. You don't want them to get crisp!

PAT the tortillas dry and add a scoop of filling to each. Roll the enchiladas and arrange in the prepared baking dish seam side down. Pour the remaining ½ cup sauce over the top.

COVER with the cheese and bake until the cheese is hot and bubbling, about 20 minutes. Garnish with the cilantro and scallions and serve with sour cream.

Empanadas

Meat and piecrust? How can you go wrong with this combo? This is one of those recipes I truly enjoy making. The idea of an empanada used to intimidate me, but as soon as I started doing my research on how to make empanadas, I wasn't so scared. I put my mind to it and just did it. I love rolling out the dough, and I use a mason jar to cut out the little rounds of dough to stuff the ground meat in. I highly recommend serving these with Trader Joe's jalapeño sauce for dipping.

MAKES ABOUT 8 EMPANADAS

prep time: 20 MINUTES   *cook time:* 35 MINUTES

2 tablespoons olive oil

1 pound lean ground beef

¼ cup diced yellow onion

1 teaspoon minced garlic

½ red bell pepper, chopped

⅓ cup canned tomato sauce

1 teaspoon chili powder

1 teaspoon ground cumin

½ teaspoon garlic powder

Salt and freshly ground black pepper

2 refrigerated piecrusts (or an equal amount of homemade pie dough)

1 egg, beaten

PREHEAT the oven to 350°F. Line a baking sheet with parchment paper.

IN a large skillet, heat 1 tablespoon of the oil over medium heat. Add the ground beef and cook, breaking it up with a wooden spoon or spatula, until browned but not completely cooked through, about 5 minutes. Remove the beef to a plate. Drain the fat out of the pan.

ADD the remaining 1 tablespoon oil to the pan, then the onion and garlic and cook until soft, 2 to 3 minutes. Return the beef to the pan, add the bell pepper, and continue to cook until the peppers soften, another 2 to 3 minutes.

POUR the tomato sauce over the meat mixture and season with the chili powder, cumin, garlic powder, and salt and black pepper to taste. Let the filling simmer for 3 to 5 minutes to blend the flavors.

REMOVE the filling from the heat to cool while you prepare the dough.

tip

After you cut out each round of dough with your mason jar, go back over it with your rolling pin, just so the dough can stretch over the filling when you fold it over and crimp with your fork.

UNROLL the dough and cut out 6 rounds about 4 inches in diameter (see Tip). Gather the scraps of dough and re-roll to cut out 2 or 3 more rounds.

ARRANGE the rounds of dough on the prepared baking sheet and add 2 heaping tablespoons of the filling to each. Fold the round in half to make a half-moon and crimp down the edges with a fork to seal. Brush the beaten egg over the tops of the empanadas.

BAKE until golden brown, 15 to 20 minutes, checking around the 12-minute mark. Remove from the oven and serve.

Fried Tacos

I know pretty much every family out there makes tacos at home, because tacos are easy and fun and delicious! But what I especially love about these tacos is the special trick I learned for frying up the tortillas in the pan.

When I was pregnant with Eric we were staying at a friend's house in Colorado and she was making tacos for dinner. She got fresh tortillas from the local grocery store and went on to show me how she liked to fry up her tortillas for her tacos. It truly made a difference, and I can't imagine having Taco Tuesday any other way now!

Some taco tips: Instead of getting the packets of taco seasoning, create your own—it will contain a lot less sodium and it's fresh from your own seasonings. You can also put your cheese and lettuce and other sides in little bowls for guests or family to dress up their tacos themselves.

MAKES 7 TO 10 TACOS

prep time: 5 MINUTES   *cook time:* 25 MINUTES

FOR THE FILLING

2 tablespoons olive oil

½ cup diced onion

1 pound ground beef

1 (10-ounce) can Ro-tel mild diced tomatoes and chilies

½ cup canned tomato sauce

1 tablespoon chili powder

¾ teaspoon ground cumin

¼ teaspoon garlic powder

¼ teaspoon onion powder

½ teaspoon salt

Freshly ground black pepper

FOR THE TACOS

Olive oil, for frying

7 to 10 (6-inch) flour tortillas (I use Trader Joe's)

Shredded Mexican cheese blend

Shredded romaine lettuce

Taco sauce or hot sauce

make the filling: In a large skillet, heat the oil over medium heat. Add the onion and sauté until translucent, 3 to 5 minutes. Add the beef and cook, breaking it apart with a wooden spoon or spatula, until browned, about 7 minutes.

DRAIN excess drippings from the pan and stir in the Ro-tel tomatoes and tomato sauce. Season with the chili powder, cumin, garlic powder, onion powder, salt, and pepper to taste.

assemble the tacos: Pour ½ inch of oil into a high-sided skillet. (You may need to add more oil after you fry the first three tortillas.) Heat over medium heat until shimmering.

WHEN the oil is ready, add a tortilla and fry for 30 seconds to a minute. Flip with tongs and fry the other side. The tortilla should puff up and begin to brown. Remove to paper towels to drain and repeat with the rest of the tortillas.

FILL the fried taco shells with a scoop of the meat mixture, then top with shredded cheese, lettuce, and taco sauce or hot sauce of your choice and fold in half before serving.

Jessie's Nachos

This is another one of those recipes that fell into my lap. I made the ground beef and beans thinking I was going to throw them on some tacos and then realized I had run out of my soft tortillas and the hard taco shells were stale. So, I searched my pantry to figure out what I could do: Can I put this on rice? Do I just serve it like Mexican chili? Then . . . there it was: I spotted a whole fresh bag of tortilla chips and boom, my nachos came to life. I laid out the chips on a pan, ladled the meat all over the top, and smothered it with Mexican cheese blend. Almost as soon as it came out of the oven, there was not one crumb left.

MAKES 6 TO 8 SERVINGS

prep time: 10 MINUTES *cook time:* 30 MINUTES

2 tablespoons olive oil

½ medium onion, diced

2 cloves garlic, chopped

1 pound ground beef

1 teaspoon garlic powder

¼ teaspoon chili powder

Salt and freshly ground black pepper

1 (14.5-ounce) can diced tomatoes, drained

1 (15-ounce) can tomato sauce

1 (4.5-ounce) can green chiles

1 (15.5-ounce) can pinto beans, rinsed and drained

1 (15.5-ounce) can black beans, rinsed and drained

FOR THE NACHOS

1 (9-ounce) bag white corn tortilla chips

3 cups shredded Mexican cheese blend

Sour cream, for serving

Chopped fresh parsley, for serving

Lime wedges, for garnish

PREHEAT the oven to 350°F.

IN a large skillet, heat the oil over medium heat. Add the onion and garlic and cook until fragrant, about 3 to 5 minutes Add the ground beef and cook, breaking it up with a wooden spoon, until browned, about 5 minutes. Drain off any excess fat.

SEASON the meat with the garlic powder, chili powder, and salt and pepper to taste. Pour in the canned tomatoes, tomato sauce, and green chiles and stir to combine. Bring to a light simmer, then add the pinto beans and black beans. Reduce the heat to medium-low and cook for 10 minutes to let the flavors come together.

assemble the nachos: Grab a large sheet pan and layer with tortilla chips. Scoop the meat and bean mixture on top and smother in the shredded cheese.

TRANSFER to the oven and bake until the cheese is all melted, about 10 minutes. Top with sour cream and parsley and garnish with lime wedges before serving.

Pork Chops

I used to be afraid of making pork chops, because it can go so wrong if you don't watch them. If you overcook pork chops they will be tough and honestly just inedible at that point. No one wants to chew that hard and give their jaws such a workout.

But with this recipe I truly feel like you can't go wrong! The flavors of apple cider and brown sugar mixed with a hint of spice from the chili powder make this an extremely flavorful, tender pork chop that will make ya feel proud when you slice right into it knowing you cooked it to perfection.

I love to serve the pork chops with yummy mashed potatoes and green beans (try my Green Beans with Almonds and Sea Salt, page 103) and corn bread on the side.

MAKES 4 TO 6 SERVINGS

prep time: **15 MINUTES**   *cook time:* **35 MINUTES**

FOR THE APPLE CIDER GLAZE

1½ cups apple cider

¼ cup pure maple syrup

1 tablespoon Dijon mustard

½ teaspoon salt

FOR THE CHOPS

2 tablespoons brown sugar

2 teaspoons chili powder

1 teaspoon garlic powder

1 teaspoon salt

½ teaspoon freshly ground black pepper

1 tablespoon olive oil

4 to 6 bone-in pork chops, about 1 inch thick

make the apple cider glaze: In a small saucepan, whisk together the cider, maple syrup, mustard, and salt and bring to a boil over medium-high heat, 3 to 4 minutes. Reduce the heat to medium-low and simmer until the cider is reduced by about half, about 10 to 15 minutes.

meanwhile, prepare the chops: In a small bowl, combine the brown sugar, chili powder, garlic powder, salt, and pepper and mix well. Stir in the oil.

PAT the chops dry with paper towels, then coat in the rub.

HEAT a large cast-iron skillet or grill pan over high heat. Once the pan is hot, working in batches, add the seasoned chops and brush with some glaze. Sear on both sides, 4 to 6 minutes per side, flipping and brushing with glaze until the chops reach an internal temperature of 145°F. (Don't take them past that point or they will get chewy.)

Sausage and Vegetable Medley Pan

quick feeds

This is a simple, to-the-point meal that even Eric knows how to make. Eric is not a big cook because it stresses him out slightly, but this is one of those that he can throw together himself. It's everything listed below, and you just throw it in a pan and voilà, you've got sausage and vegetables, baby!

MAKES 4 SERVINGS

prep time: 10 MINUTES   *cook time:* 30 MINUTES

1 cup thickly sliced red onion

2 cups sliced baby potatoes

2 cups small broccoli florets

8 ounces green beans (about 1½ cups)

2 cups sliced precooked sausage

1 tablespoon olive oil

1 teaspoon Italian seasoning

Salt and freshly ground black pepper

PREHEAT the oven to 375°F. Line a large sheet pan with foil or parchment paper.

IN a large bowl, toss the onion, potatoes, broccoli, green beans, sausage, oil, and Italian seasoning. Add a dash of salt and pepper and spread out on the prepared sheet pan.

ROAST until the vegetables are tender and the sausage is browning, 20 to 30 minutes, tossing halfway through.

For the Birds

Chicken or turkey is the centerpiece of many of my meals, simply because I always know what I'm going to get! No surprises like there can be with cooking fish or steak and pork that can get tough or overdone. It's hard to mess up chicken or turkey, because they are so easy to cook. They are always in my fridge ready to inspire me to be creative and whip up something new or just to make a simple recipe that I've been cooking for years. I typically have ground chicken and ground turkey in my fridge, because they are easy to freeze if we decide to go out of town or make something else. I don't like to waste food, so ground meat allows me to keep it fresh. I have for you in this chapter many amazing chicken and turkey recipes that I think y'all are going to just LOVE!

Roasted Chicken and Vegetables

This is one of those easy-to-fix chicken recipes. I love how you can lay out all the ingredients listed below and spread them on a pan, pop it in the oven, and be done.

This is one of Eric's favorites, being a big meat and potatoes kinda guy. The Italian seasoning with the chopped fresh herbs really gives it a unique flavor. This is great for fall meals, too, with the added fresh rosemary.

MAKES 3 OR 4 SERVINGS

3 pounds baby potatoes, halved

1 medium red onion, sliced

¼ cup olive oil

Salt and freshly cracked black pepper

1 whole chicken (3 to 4 pounds)

½ teaspoon Italian seasoning

1 sprig fresh rosemary

1 large carrot, peeled

2 stalks celery

4 cloves garlic, peeled

8 tablespoons (1 stick) unsalted butter

2 tablespoons Chicken Rub (recipe follows) or store-bought chicken seasoning

Chicken Rub

MAKES A SCANT ½ CUP

1 tablespoon paprika

1 tablespoon sea salt

3 tablespoons garlic powder

1 tablespoon freshly ground black pepper

1 tablespoon dried parsley

1½ teaspoons dried thyme

prep time: 30 MINUTES   *cook time:* 2 HOURS

PREHEAT the oven to 400°F.

ARRANGE the potatoes and onion in the bottom of a large baking pan or roaster and drizzle with 2 tablespoons of the oil. Season with salt and pepper to taste and toss to coat.

SET the chicken on top. Brush the chicken with the remaining 2 tablespoons olive oil and generously season the skin and cavity with the Italian seasoning and salt and pepper. Insert the rosemary, carrot, celery stalks, garlic, and ½ stick of butter in the cavity. Gently press the remaining ½ stick butter under the skin, being careful not to pierce the skin too much. Season the chicken with the rub.

TRANSFER to the oven and roast until the chicken reaches an internal temperature of 165°F, 1½ to 2 hours. Remove from the oven and serve.

COMBINE all the ingredients in a small bowl and mix well. Store in an airtight container until ready to use.

Honey Fried Chicken

I mean did ya really think I wouldn't have fried chicken in my debut cookbook? I am from the South, so I had to include one of that region's true delicacies. I remember being in high school sneaking away on lunch breaks to go to the drive-through at Church's Chicken to order fried chicken, mashed potatoes, biscuits, and fried okra . . . ahh those were the days. All that food and I wouldn't gain an ounce.

Anyway . . . I won't eat fried chicken unless it's on the bone. I find tenders to be boring and dry. I want the bone because it's always more flavorful and juicier and more fun. This is my favorite fried chicken recipe, with a little bit of honey to top it off. Serve the chicken with warm biscuits.

MAKES 4 TO 6 SERVINGS

prep time: 3 HOURS   *cook time:* 30 MINUTES

10 pieces of chicken
  (2 drumsticks, 2 thighs,
  4 breast halves, and 2 wings),
  unless you are like me
  and want to eat only the
  drumsticks, then get more
  drumsticks!

1 tablespoon plus 2 teaspoons
  salt

1½ tablespoons black pepper

4 cups buttermilk

Vegetable or canola oil, for
  deep-frying

4 cups all-purpose flour

3 tablespoons garlic powder

2 tablespoons onion powder

1 teaspoon paprika

1 teaspoon Tony Chachere's
  Creole Seasoning

1 cup honey

SEASON the chicken with 1 tablespoon of the salt and 1 tablespoon of the pepper. Place in a large bowl and cover with the buttermilk. Marinate in the refrigerator for a few hours or overnight.

POUR 3 to 4 inches of oil into a large deep pot or Dutch oven. Heat over medium-high heat until the oil reaches 350°F.

IN a large bowl, use a fork to stir together the flour, garlic powder, onion powder, paprika, Tony's seasoning, and the remaining 2 teaspoons salt and ½ tablespoon pepper.

REMOVE the chicken from the buttermilk (discard the marinade) and dredge in the flour mixture. Arrange on a baking sheet while you prepare to fry.

WORKING in batches, drop the coated chicken pieces into the hot oil and cook until golden brown, 7 to 10 minutes depending on the size. Transfer to a wire rack, then drizzle with the honey.

Game Day Grilled Chicken Wings

On football game days we make chili and we make chicken wings. I think it's actually a sin to not make either on such an important day in America (jk lol). But seriously, these wings are so finger-lickin' good and so easy to throw together. What I love is that the flavor isn't too heavy and they aren't too messy with all that extra sauce. Keep it simple and get your ranch dip ready for dipping!

MAKES 4 TO 6 SERVINGS

prep time: 1 HOUR   *cook time:* 15 MINUTES

½ cup olive oil, plus more for the grill pan, if using

1 tablespoon garlic powder

1 tablespoon mustard powder

1 teaspoon ground cumin

Dash of Tony Chachere's Creole Seasoning

Salt and freshly ground black pepper

3 pounds chicken wings

IN a small bowl, whisk together the oil, garlic powder, mustard powder, cumin, Tony's seasoning, and salt and pepper to taste. Add the wings to a sturdy resealable plastic bag, pour in the oil mixture, toss to coat, and refrigerate for 1 hour.

HEAT an outdoor grill or oiled grill pan to medium heat.

ADD the wings and cook, turning occasionally, until they are cooked through and the skin is crispy, about 15 minutes.

Stuffed Chicken Parmesan

Eric and I share a love of food, but since he doesn't really cook for the most part, he typically makes a lot of food requests of me. And he's very vocal about it. (Well, it's because I have spoiled him, but I don't mind it since I love to cook.)

One day I thought he was about to have a serious talk with me about something deep and I sat there patiently wondering what he was going to say. As he opened his mouth to share with me this big emotional statement I thought was coming, he said calmly, "Jess, you don't ever make Chicken Parmesan and it's honestly one of my favorite things to eat and I wish you would make it." Ummmm, what??? I wanted to bust out laughing so hard as I looked at his sweet serious face, but I held it in, took a deep breath, smiled, and said, "You got it, babe. I will get right on that."

So here it is, Eric darling, your chicken Parm, and it's damn good. This stuffed chicken Parmesan couldn't be easier! Season, slice, stuff, coat, and bake.

MAKES 4 SERVINGS

prep time: 10 MINUTES   *cook time:* 25 MINUTES

FOR THE CHICKEN

4 boneless, skinless chicken breasts (6 ounces each)

8 ounces fresh mozzarella cheese, sliced into 8 pieces

1 cup all-purpose flour

2 large eggs, lightly beaten

1 cup panko bread crumbs

2 tablespoons olive oil, for frying

½ cup freshly shaved Parmesan cheese

prepare the chicken: Place the chicken breasts on a cutting board and pound with a rolling pin or the smooth side of a meat pounder to even the thickness to ¾ inch. Starting on the meatier side of a breast, use a sharp knife to cut a pocket into the center of the meat (don't go all the way through) to make room for the sliced mozzarella. Place 1 slice of mozzarella in each pocket.

SET up a dredging station: Place the flour in a shallow bowl. Place the eggs in a second bowl and the panko in a third. Dredge the stuffed chicken in the flour on both sides, then in the egg, followed by the panko. Make sure the whole chicken is covered to prevent the cheese from leaking out during baking.

PREHEAT the oven to 425°F.

IN a large cast-iron skillet, heat the oil over medium heat. Lay the breaded chicken in the hot pan and brown the chicken for 2 to 3 minutes on each side.

FOR THE ARUGULA SALAD

4 cups baby arugula

½ cup sliced grape tomatoes

Shaved Parmesan cheese

Salt and freshly ground black pepper

Homemade Go-To Salad Dressing (page 45)

ARRANGE the browned chicken in a baking dish and layer with the remaining 4 slices of mozzarella.

TRANSFER to the oven and bake for 15 to 20 minutes. Turn the broiler to high, sprinkle the chicken with the shaved Parmesan, and broil until the cheese is bubbling and browned, about 1 minute.

make the arugula salad: In a large bowl, toss the arugula, tomatoes, and shaved Parmesan. Season with salt and pepper to taste and lightly drizzle with dressing.

SERVE the chicken over the arugula salad.

Tex-Mex Casserole

I would love to tell you that I sat in my kitchen, closed my eyes, and dreamed up this Mexican chicken casserole, but that would be a lie. The truth is, I was making chicken tacos and had everything simmering in the pan on the stove. The chicken was cooked with the black beans and the corn, and the sauce was all ready as I was stirring it so proudly. I went to my refrigerator to pull out my tortillas when I realized they were two weeks expired. I thought to myself, Crap, what am I going to do now?

That's when I decided I would take out the frozen white rice and combine it with all this goodness on the stove, throw it in a glass pan, cover it with cheese, and voilà, Mexican chicken casserole.

Eric came in to smell the fabulousness and asked me where the tacos were, and I told him that I had changed my mind and decided to make him a special casserole. He never really found out the truth until now, which doesn't matter because he was so happy with his Mexican chicken casserole. In fact, he told me to "add it to the book."

MAKES 6 TO 8 SERVINGS

prep time: 20 MINUTES   *cook time:* 45 MINUTES

1 tablespoon avocado oil

½ cup chopped onion

3 cloves garlic, minced

1 (15-ounce) can black beans, rinsed and drained

3 cups frozen white rice

1 (4.5-ounce) can green chiles

1 (15-ounce) can tomato sauce

1 (12-ounce) bag frozen white corn kernels

2 cups shredded rotisserie chicken

1 teaspoon chili powder

1 teaspoon ground cumin

1 teaspoon garlic powder

1 teaspoon onion powder

Salt and freshly ground black pepper

2 cups shredded low-fat Mexican Four Cheese Blend

1 cup sour cream

Sliced scallions, for garnish

PREHEAT the oven to 375°F.

IN a large pot, heat the oil over medium heat. Add the onion and garlic and sauté until translucent, 3 to 5 minutes. Add the beans, rice, chiles, tomato sauce, corn, and shredded chicken and stir to combine. Stir in the chili powder, cumin, garlic powder, onion powder, and salt and pepper to taste. Cover and let that simmer for about 5 minutes, until the rice is warmed and the sauce is hot.

POUR the mixture into a 3-quart glass baking dish, cover with foil, and bake until the rice is tender, about 30 minutes.

UNCOVER, top with the cheese, and bake until the cheese is melted, about 5 minutes longer.

SMEAR the sour cream on top and garnish with sliced scallions before serving.

Ground Chicken Asian Stir-Fry

I love cooking shows and documentaries about food, because I'm always looking for more ways to educate myself in the kitchen. After watching one show in particular, I couldn't believe I had been missing out on this magical thing called coconut aminos. It tastes very similar to soy sauce but doesn't have all that crazy sodium. And frankly, I think it tastes better. So get your coconut aminos ready for this recipe.

This one gets the "quick feeds" stamp as one of those meals you can throw together in 20 minutes for hungry babies. If you want to skip over some more steps, there are many grocery stores that have bags of frozen pre-cut Asian or stir-fry vegetables. This dish is so good and hearty and your babies will enjoy it, too.

MAKES 4 SERVINGS

prep time: **15 MINUTES**   *cook time:* **20 MINUTES**

2 tablespoons olive oil

½ cup diced white onion

3 cloves garlic, minced

1 pound lean ground chicken

½ teaspoon garlic powder

1 teaspoon onion powder

2 cups chopped broccoli florets

1 cup diced carrots

½ green bell pepper, sliced into strips

½ red bell pepper, sliced into strips

½ cup snow peas

½ cup sliced button mushrooms

¼ cup canned sliced bamboo shoots

½ cup canned baby corn

2 tablespoons coconut aminos or soy sauce

1 large egg

Salt and freshly ground black pepper

2 cups cooked white rice, for serving

IN a large skillet or wok, heat the oil over medium heat. Add the onion, garlic, and ground chicken and sauté until the chicken begins to brown, 7 to 10 minutes. Season with the garlic powder and onion powder.

ADD the broccoli, carrots, bell peppers, snow peas, mushrooms, bamboo shoots, baby corn, and coconut aminos to the pan and stir-fry until the carrots are tender, about 5 minutes.

CRACK the egg into the center of the veggies and lightly scramble until no liquid egg remains, 1 to 3 minutes. Season with salt and pepper.

SERVE over the white rice.

Chicken Chili

Another chili recipe, you ask? OK, listen, it was hard for me to not include all my chili recipes. I have about ten more up my sleeve, but I'll save them for next time. This one is different thanks to the sweetness I add to it. This is the perfect pot of chili to make during the fall.

MAKES 6 TO 8 SERVINGS

prep time: 10 MINUTES   *cook time:* 45 MINUTES

1 tablespoon extra-virgin olive oil

½ large white onion, roughly chopped

2 cloves garlic, finely chopped

1½ tablespoons chili powder

2 teaspoons dried oregano

1 teaspoon ground cumin

1 teaspoon ground coriander

¼ teaspoon cayenne pepper, or to taste

Pinch of ground cinnamon

Pinch of sugar

1 pound ground chicken breast

1 (15-ounce) can tomato sauce

1 cup water

½ cup mild or medium salsa

1 cup frozen yellow corn kernels

1 (4.5-ounce) can green chiles

1 (15-ounce) can chickpeas, rinsed and drained

1 (16-ounce) can navy beans, rinsed and drained

Salt

⅓ cup chopped fresh cilantro

Sliced avocado, for garnish

Mexican Four Cheese Blend, for garnish

Tortilla chips, for serving

IN a large soup pot or Dutch oven, heat the oil over medium heat. Add the onion and garlic and cook for about 5 minutes, stirring frequently, until the onion is translucent.

STIR in the chili powder, oregano, cumin, coriander, cayenne, cinnamon, and sugar and cook for 1 minute, stirring constantly.

ADD the chicken. Stir to break up and brown for 3 minutes. Add the tomato sauce, water, salsa, corn, green chiles, chickpeas, and navy beans. Season with salt to taste, then bring to a boil over high heat. Reduce the heat to medium-low to simmer, cover, and cook for about 20 minutes, stirring often, until the flavors have melded and the chili is thick.

STIR in the cilantro right before serving. Garnish with sliced avocado and Mexican cheese blend. Serve with tortilla chips.

Spicy Turkey Chili

If you like spicy chili, then I double dog dare you to make this recipe! I love anything spicy and can handle pretty much any heat thrown my way. Now I'm not saying this one is so spicy that you will have tears coming down your face, but it definitely has a kick and I wouldn't recommend making it for your kids—even though my kids don't seem fazed by the heat, probably because they grew up on it.

I love this chili in particular, not only because of the spice but also because of the added chickpeas and lentils. It switches things up and makes it a little fancier than your regular beef and bean chili, especially when you garnish it with the parsley on top.

MAKES 4 SERVINGS

prep time: 15 MINUTES   *cook time:* 50 MINUTES

1 tablespoon olive oil

1 medium yellow onion, diced

1 cup diced carrots (about 2 carrots)

1 cup chopped celery (about 2 stalks)

½ red bell pepper, diced

½ yellow bell pepper, diced

2 cloves garlic, minced

1 jalapeño, minced

1 pound lean ground turkey

1 (14.5-ounce) can diced tomatoes

1 (6-ounce) can tomato paste

2 (15-ounce) cans chickpeas, rinsed and drained

1 cup dried lentils

1 tablespoon chili powder

2 teaspoons ground cumin

½ teaspoon paprika

Chopped fresh parsley, for garnish

Shredded white Cheddar cheese, for serving

IN a large pot or Dutch oven, heat the oil over medium heat. Add the onion, carrots, celery, and bell peppers and cook until soft, about 5 minutes. Add the garlic and jalapeño and continue to cook for another 2 minutes.

ADD the turkey and cook over medium heat until browned, 6 to 8 minutes, breaking it up with a wooden spoon or spatula. Stir in the diced tomatoes, tomato paste, chickpeas, and lentils. Fill a 15-ounce can (from the chickpeas) with water and add it to the pot. Stir in the chili powder, cumin, and paprika. Reduce the heat to medium-low. Cover and simmer, stirring occasionally, until the lentils are tender, about 45 minutes.

GARNISH with parsley and serve with shredded Cheddar.

Moist Maker Turkey Sandwich

Yes, this is a Friends reference and I think everyone should have a "moist maker" at least once in their life. Every time I watch this episode, I want my own turkey moist maker sandwich. I know in the show they added an extra slice of bread, but I don't need the extra bread. I'm all about the meat! So, here is my "Friend"-ly version of it.

MAKES 1 SANDWICH

prep time: 5 MINUTES   *cook time:* 10 MINUTES

1 cup shredded leftover turkey

½ cup leftover turkey gravy

1 tablespoon unsalted butter

2 slices white bread

2 to 3 tablespoons cranberry sauce, from a can or leftovers

IN a small pan, heat up the turkey and stir in the gravy.

WHILE the turkey cooks, butter the bread and lightly grill it in a hot skillet.

SPREAD the cranberry sauce on both slices of the bread, and fill the sandwich with the hot turkey and gravy.

Seafood (Mermaid Food)

There is nothing better than fresh shrimp from the Gulf, or a nice beer-battered fish with French fries on a patio overlooking the ocean. We have a home in Florida on the water and I have to be real when I explain to you that yes, I get very excited about going to the beach, but I get equally excited about all the seafood I know I'm going to devour when I get there.

Seafood Gumbo

When I'm asked what my favorite thing to eat is, I blurt it out no questions asked: GUMBO! I love gumbo more than anything. I could eat it every day for a week (and I've actually done that before). Of course, it's the most delicious meal I've ever had in my life, but it's also therapeutic to make, stirring the roux with my big wooden spoon as it becomes fragrant. I love each step and watching the flavors come together. I've been eating gumbo for as long as I can remember living. It was just something you ate growing up having a family from Louisiana. Making gumbo makes me feel connected to my family and proud of those Louisiana roots.

I know gumbo can seem a little scary and intimidating, but I promise you if you follow my steps you can make it, too. Roll up your sleeves and get to peeling the shrimp, cher' bebe.

MAKES 8 TO 10 SERVINGS

prep time: 15 MINUTES   *cook time:* 3 HOURS

1 cup all-purpose flour

1 cup olive or canola oil

1 medium yellow onion, chopped

1 cup chopped celery

1 green bell pepper, chopped

1 (10-ounce) can Ro-tel diced tomatoes

4 cloves garlic, minced

3 pounds wild-caught Gulf shrimp

4 clusters crab legs

8 ounces canned lump crabmeat

1 (14-ounce) package smoked sausage, sliced and cooked

1 tablespoon Worcestershire sauce

1 teaspoon cayenne pepper, or to taste

2 teaspoons filé powder, or to taste

3 cups frozen sliced okra

3 scallions, chopped

Salt and freshly ground black pepper

Tony Chachere's Creole Seasoning

Cooked white rice, for serving

IN a large Dutch oven or other heavy-bottomed pot, combine the flour and oil and stir constantly with a wooden spoon over medium heat until the roux turns a rich dark brown. This can take anywhere from 20 to 30 minutes, depending on how dark you like your roux to be (I prefer mine dark). Be careful not to burn the mixture. Do not leave the pot or the spoon unattended, or you might have to start again.

TO the roux, add the onion, celery, and bell pepper and cook over medium heat until soft, about 5 minutes. Slowly add 2 quarts water, stirring until incorporated. Add the canned tomatoes and bring to a simmer. Add the garlic, shrimp, crab legs, crabmeat, smoked sausage, Worcestershire sauce, cayenne, and filé. Simmer over low heat for at least 2 hours or up to 4 hours.

ADD the okra, scallions, and salt, pepper, and Tony's seasoning to taste. Keep over low heat until ready to eat. Serve over white rice.

"I love each step and watching the flavors come together."

Seafood Boil

I love me a good seafood boil in the summer! This is a party in a pot and something folks down South, especially in Louisiana, do year-round. It's the best when crawfish is in season, but if it's not, shrimp and crab will do just fine.

Throw all the ingredients in a pot with seasoning and corn and smoked sausage like a true Cajun would. Get your newspapers out and lay them all on a wooden table outside, then dump the pot on the newspapers and get to peelin' and eatin' with a group of friends and family.

MAKES 6 TO 8 SERVINGS

prep time: 5 MINUTES   *cook time:* 25 MINUTES

Salt (lots)

½ cup Old Bay Seasoning, plus more for garnish

8 cloves garlic, peeled

1 large onion, peeled and cut into 6 wedges

4 lemons, halved

1 pound small Yukon Gold potatoes, halved

5 ears corn, cut into 3- to 4-inch pieces

1 pound smoked pork sausage (preferably kielbasa or andouille), cut into 1-inch lengths

1 pound king crab legs

2 pounds shrimp, peeled and deveined, tails on

1 cup unsalted butter, melted, for serving

FILL a large pot three-quarters full with water. Season generously with salt and add the Old Bay, garlic, onion, and lemons. Bring to a rolling boil over high heat.

ONCE boiling, add the potatoes and cook for 10 minutes.

ADD the corn, sausage, and crab legs and cook for 10 minutes. Add the shrimp. Once everything is cooked through, strain and lay the seafood on newspapers across a wooden table (preferably outside so nothing gets dirty). Serve with the melted butter. Dig in.

Coconut Curry Shrimp

I almost put this one in Just Jessie, but we ran out of space in the recipe section so I decided to save it just in case I got the opportunity to have my own cookbook. And, well, dreams do come true! I'm glad I saved it because now I can share it with y'all. I've been making this one for a while. I love the Indian influence with the curry and of course the shrimp soaked in the sauce. Even though I have been making this for years, I didn't try adding bok choy until recently. It turned out great, and now this is one of my sister's favorite dishes!

MAKES 4 SERVINGS

prep time: 5 MINUTES   *cook time:* 20 MINUTES

2 tablespoons unsalted butter

1½ pounds shrimp, peeled and deveined

Salt and freshly ground black pepper

1 tablespoon olive oil

1 medium onion, chopped

4 cloves garlic, minced

1 (13.5-ounce) can full-fat coconut milk

2 tablespoons honey

1 tablespoon curry powder

Bok choy (optional)

Cooked white rice, for serving

Chopped fresh cilantro, for garnish

IN a large skillet, heat the butter over medium heat. Add the shrimp and sauté until they just begin to turn pink, about 5 minutes. Season with salt and pepper to taste and remove to a plate.

IN the same pan, heat the oil over medium-low. Add the onion and garlic and sauté until the garlic is fragrant and the onion is translucent, 2 to 3 minutes. Whisk in the coconut milk, honey, and curry powder. Bring to a simmer over medium heat and cook until the sauce begins to thicken, about 5 minutes. (You can add bok choy to the pan if you want to add some greens to your curry. Cook 'til tender!)

RETURN the shrimp to the pan and toss to coat in the sauce. Serve over white rice and garnish with chopped cilantro.

Mama's Crawfish Étouffée

Crawfish étouffée is a family favorite and one of those recipes my mom nails every time. This is her personal recipe, and I wanted her to say a little something about it:

Jess and Sydney were in the kitchen cooking with me since as soon as they could sit up in a highchair. Actually, before that, I would prop them up on my hip and stir my pot with my other hand. It's just what you do, at least where I'm from down in South Louisiana where the people and food are full of flavor.

Crawfish étouffée is a prime example of that. My take on this yummy Creole dish will warm the soul and the belly. Don't be afraid to try crawfish. They are a favorite in our family. Even the Yankee boys me and Jessie married love our Cajun and Creole dishes. My husband, Steve, prefers his crawfish étouffée over fried catfish instead of rice. We call this Catfish Atchafalaya.

I hope you try this dish, but be prepared, once you've had a taste of the South you'll never want to go back.

Love, Mama

MAKES 4 SERVINGS

prep time: 15 MINUTES   *cook time:* 40 MINUTES

6 tablespoons unsalted butter

1 (4-ounce) can portobello mushrooms, drained

2 large stalks celery, chopped

½ onion, chopped

2 tablespoons all-purpose flour

1 (10-ounce) can Ro-tel mild diced tomatoes and green chilies

2 squirts Worcestershire sauce (about ½ teaspoon)

1 pound crawfish tails

2 scallions, sliced

1 teaspoon minced garlic

2 bay leaves

Salt and black pepper

Tony Chachere's Creole Seasoning

Handful of chopped fresh parsley

Cooked white rice or fried catfish, for serving

IN a large skillet, melt the butter. Add the mushrooms, celery, and onions and sauté over medium-low heat until the celery and onions soften, about 5 minutes. Sprinkle in the flour, mix well, and cook about 15 minutes, stirring until thickened. Add the tomatoes, 2½ cups water, the Worcestershire sauce, crawfish tails, scallions, garlic, bay leaves, and salt, pepper, and Tony's seasoning to taste. Simmer until the crawfish are cooked through, 10 to 20 minutes.

STIR in the parsley and serve over cooked rice or fried catfish.

Salmon Fillet with Asparagus

The flavor of this salmon really surprises me every time. I always forget how good it is until I make it. It's one of my recipes that is underrated and that I should really shout out more. The marinade is the only part that takes awhile because you really do want the flavors to come together. Once it's marinated, you toss the salmon in the oven with asparagus and sliced golden cut potatoes and cook them to perfection.

MAKES 3 OR 4 SERVINGS

prep time: 2 HOURS   *cook time:* 15 MINUTES

2 tablespoons unsalted butter, melted and cooled

2 tablespoons pure maple syrup

1½ tablespoons spicy brown mustard

1 tablespoon apple cider vinegar

1 teaspoon olive oil

½ teaspoon paprika

Salt and freshly ground black pepper

Cooking spray, for the pan (optional)

1 pound salmon fillets

1 bunch asparagus, tough ends trimmed

IN a small bowl, whisk together the butter, maple syrup, mustard, vinegar, oil, paprika, and salt and pepper to taste. Place the salmon fillets in a large resealable plastic bag or dish and cover with the marinade. Refrigerate for at least 2 hours or overnight.

PREHEAT the oven to 375°F. Line a sheet pan with parchment paper or coat with cooking spray.

ARRANGE the asparagus on the prepared pan, then top with the marinated salmon fillets. Brush with any leftover marinade and discard the rest.

BAKE until the asparagus is tender and the fish just flakes, 12 to 15 minutes. Season with more salt and pepper to taste before serving.

Shrimp Po'Boy

Shrimp po'boys are a classic in Louisiana! I remember going through drive-throughs picking up our po'boys and not understanding why no other places in the country had a drive-through po'boy situation. Louisiana has a mind of its own. They even have drive-through daiquiri stations and snow cone stands everywhere. Fun fact: It's the only state that still has parishes and not counties. It really was a cool place to be able to live and frequent growing up since my whole family was born and raised there. Whenever I would order a shrimp po'boy at a restaurant outside Louisiana it would just disappoint me, so I stopped. There ain't nothing like a true Louisiana shrimp po'boy and I was lucky enough to be taught how to make 'em just right. So, get your French bread ready and your cornmeal fish fry and laissez les bons temps rouler!

MAKES 4 OR 6 SERVINGS

prep time: 10 MINUTES   *cook time:* 25 MINUTES

FOR THE SHRIMP

Canola oil, for deep-frying

1 cup Zatarain's Wonderful Fish Fri

2 pounds peeled and deveined wild-caught shrimp

⅓ cup yellow mustard

Tony Chachere's Creole Seasoning

Salt and freshly ground black pepper

FOR SERVING

2 or 3 loaves French bread, split horizontally and cut in half

Mayonnaise

Yellow mustard

Shredded lettuce

Sliced tomato

cook the shrimp: Pour 2 inches of canola oil into a large pot and turn the heat to medium while you prepare the shrimp.

SPREAD the Zatarain's fish fry mixture in a shallow bowl. Coat the shrimp in the mustard, then smother in the fish fry mixture and place on a plate.

WHEN the oil reaches 350°F, fry 4 or 5 shrimp at a time until golden brown, 2 to 3 minutes. Transfer to paper towels to drain. Season the fried shrimp with Tony's seasoning, salt, and pepper to taste.

to serve: Slather each piece of bread with mayonnaise and mustard. Top with lettuce, tomato, and the fried shrimp.

Asian Salmon

I was always scared and confused by sushi, but I would still go to sushi restaurants with my friends or with Eric and would either order the chicken teriyaki or salmon. I would watch my friends with their chopsticks eating their bits of ginger and dipping their sushi in soy sauce while I dug in with my fork eating my well-cooked salmon. (I'm proud to say now I have expanded my palate and will get into some cooked sushi and maybe a few rolls with some raw salmon from time to time.) But it's thanks to being dragged to all of those sushi spots for years that I developed my love of cooked salmon. Here is my Asian-inspired salmon recipe.

MAKES 3 OR 4 SERVINGS

prep time: 2 HOURS   *cook time:* 15 MINUTES

¼ cup soy sauce

2 tablespoons olive oil

1 tablespoon apple cider vinegar

1 tablespoon pure maple syrup or honey

1 tablespoon Dijon mustard

¼ teaspoon garlic powder

¼ teaspoon onion powder

Cooking spray, for the pan (optional)

3 or 4 salmon fillets (about 1 pound total)

IN a small bowl, combine the soy sauce, oil, vinegar, maple syrup, mustard, garlic powder, and onion powder. Place the salmon in a large resealable plastic bag or dish and cover with the marinade. Refrigerate for at least 2 hours or overnight.

PREHEAT the oven to 375°F. Line a sheet pan with parchment paper or coat with cooking spray.

ARRANGE the salmon on the prepared pan and baste with the marinade. Bake until the salmon just flakes, 12 to 15 minutes. Remove from the oven and serve.

Fish 'n' Chips

My mouth waters thinking about this beer-battered cod and chips recipe I'm about to share with y'all. The coating on this is to die for and so is the added beer flavor. Get your tartar sauce and your favorite draft beer ready and dive in.

MAKES 4 TO 6 SERVINGS

prep time: 20 MINUTES   *cook time:* 25 MINUTES

FOR THE CHIPS

½ teaspoon smoked paprika

½ teaspoon dried parsley

½ teaspoon Italian seasoning

½ teaspoon onion salt

¼ teaspoon garlic powder

⅛ teaspoon freshly ground
  black pepper

Pinch of cayenne pepper

2 russet (baking) potatoes

FOR THE BEER-BATTERED FISH

¼ cup all-purpose flour

¼ cup white cornmeal

½ teaspoon garlic powder

¼ teaspoon smoked paprika

½ teaspoon Tony Chachere's
  Creole Seasoning

Sea salt and freshly ground
  black pepper

1 teaspoon unsalted butter,
  melted

1 large egg, beaten

1 egg white, beaten until stiff

½ cup beer

Canola oil, for deep-frying

2 pounds frozen cod fillets,
  thawed and patted dry

Lemon wedges, for serving

prepare the chips: In a small bowl, combine the smoked paprika, parsley, Italian seasoning, onion salt, garlic powder, black pepper, and cayenne. Slice the potatoes into thin strips.

make the beer-battered fish: In a large bowl, whisk together the flour, cornmeal, garlic powder, smoked paprika, Tony's seasoning, and salt and pepper to taste. Stir in the melted butter, beaten whole egg, and beaten egg white. Gently stir in the beer. Cover and let rest for 10 minutes to activate the batter.

POUR 4 inches of oil into a Dutch oven. Heat over medium-high heat until the oil reaches a temperature of 350°F on a deep fry or candy thermometer. Next, dip the cod in the batter to coat. Working in batches, plunge it in the hot oil and fry until golden, 4 to 6 minutes. Repeat with the remaining fish.

CONTINUING to work in batches, fry the potatoes in the hot oil until golden, 4 to 7 minutes. Remove to paper towels and dust with the chip seasoning. Serve with lemon wedges.

SEAFOOD (MERMAID FOOD)

Fit-Friendly Meals

Y'all know how much I love food and that I love to indulge, but I also like to maintain a healthy life and keep my body fit. I ask myself, though, why should we skimp on good food when trying to tone things up or have a healthy lifestyle? It's all about portion control for me. Instead of having an entire big bowl of pasta maybe I will have half the amount I would typically eat if I was indulging. I think if we just cut our portions in half once in a while we would see or maintain the results we're looking for.

I do have moments when I want to get ready for a photo shoot or lose a couple pounds before hitting the red carpet for an event, but don't want to skimp on any good food while doing so. When trying to lose some weight and tone up, I maintain a diet heavy on protein and good vegetables and low in carbs. Here are a couple of examples of a "fitten-ish" day, filled with a few of my recipes that I like to incorporate daily when I've got a personal goal:

Day 1

BREAKFAST: *Coffee and 2 slices of wheat toast with butter*

LUNCH: *Grilled chicken over arugula salad with my Homemade Go-To Salad Dressing (page 45)*

SNACK: *1 Oat Protein Ball (page 195)*

DINNER: *Chicken Cauliflower Bowl (page 193)*

Day 2

BREAKFAST: *Coffee and 1 whole wheat English muffin with butter*

LUNCH: *Ground Turkey Sweet Potato Skillet (page 191)*

SNACK: *1 Oat Protein Ball (page 195)*

DINNER: *Ground Chicken Lettuce Cups (page 197)*

Ground Turkey Sweet Potato Skillet

I created this recipe years ago and it's been a favorite ever since. So many of my family and friends have called me for this recipe in particular and now they won't have to because I'm sharing it!

I remember so clearly the day I made this. I was long overdue for a grocery store run. All I had left in the house was ground turkey, a bag of spinach for salad, cheese, and sweet potatoes. So, I diced up some onions I had in the pantry, threw them in a pan, added the ground turkey and seasoning, and threw the whole bag of spinach in. I kept on going until I finished it off with some shredded reduced-fat mozzarella cheese that I had. Eric loved it so much he started asking for it every week, and so did anyone else in my family who had tried it. I knew it was a hit! On top of it just being delicious, it's a bodybuilder's dream meal. It's the perfect meal for when you're working out and building muscle and still trying to keep it lean!

MAKES 4 SERVINGS

prep time: **10 MINUTES**   *cook time:* **30 MINUTES**

2 tablespoons olive oil

2 large sweet potatoes, peeled and diced

½ cup diced yellow onion

1 pound lean ground turkey

1 teaspoon salt, plus more to taste

¼ teaspoon freshly ground black pepper, plus more to taste

1 (16-ounce) bag spinach

1 teaspoon garlic powder

½ teaspoon onion powder

½ cup shredded mozzarella cheese

IN a large skillet, heat 1 tablespoon of the oil over medium heat. Add the sweet potatoes and onion and cook until the onion has softened, 3 to 5 minutes. Add the ground turkey, salt, and pepper. Continue to cook, stirring frequently, until the ground turkey is cooked through and the sweet potatoes are tender, 8 to 10 minutes.

ADD the entire bag of spinach, one handful at a time. Drizzle with the remaining 1 tablespoon olive oil and season with the garlic powder, onion powder, and more salt and pepper. Cover the pot and cook over low heat for 10 minutes, until the spinach is wilted and the sweet potatoes are soft.

JUST before serving, sprinkle the mozzarella over the entire top, cover the pan, and cook until it melts. Serve hot.

Chicken Cauliflower Bowl

I was so happy when cauliflower rice became a popular trend, because I love everything about it: the texture, the flavor, and the fact that it's a smarter way to eat if you want to avoid a lot of grains and carbs. I'm sticking with it even if the trend goes away.

I know this recipe might seem a little overwhelming with all its steps, but it's worth it because the calories are so low that it's totally guilt-free.

MAKES 1 OR 2 SERVINGS

prep time: 1 HOUR   *cook time:* 1 HOUR

4 ounces chicken breast tenders

1 tablespoon fresh lemon juice

1 clove garlic, minced

½ teaspoon dried thyme

⅓ cup broccoli florets

1 ounce yellow squash, thickly sliced

1 ounce zucchini, thickly sliced

1 ounce red bell pepper, cut into strips

1 ounce yellow bell pepper, cut into strips

1 ounce red onions, sliced

2 to 4 tablespoons chicken broth

3 ounces cauliflower rice, frozen or fresh

2 tablespoons olive oil

Salt and freshly ground black pepper

2 jarred grilled marinated artichoke hearts

2 slices yellow tomato

1 tablespoon store-bought lemon-garlic aioli

IN a medium bowl, toss the chicken with the lemon juice, garlic, and thyme to coat and marinate for at least 30 minutes or overnight in the refrigerator.

PREHEAT the oven to 350°F.

IN a large ovenproof skillet or on a sheet pan, arrange the broccoli, squash, zucchini, bell peppers, and onions. Drizzle the vegetables with the chicken broth and bake until they are tender and beginning to brown, 35 to 40 minutes, tossing halfway through.

MEANWHILE, in a cast-iron skillet, heat 1 tablespoon of the oil over medium-high heat. Cook the chicken, turning once, until cooked through, 5 to 7 minutes on each side. Let sit for a couple of minutes, then slice and set aside.

IF using frozen cauliflower rice, steam according to the package directions and toss with the remaining 1 tablespoon oil. If using fresh, heat the oil in a skillet, add the cauliflower, and heat until it begins to soften. Season the cooked cauliflower rice with salt and pepper to taste.

BUILD the bowl(s) in this order: cauliflower rice, roasted veggies, sliced chicken, artichoke hearts, and sliced tomato. Drizzle with the aioli before serving.

Oat Protein Balls

One day Eric asked me to make some protein bars that he could snack on between practices. I scanned the pantry and started pulling things off the shelves and this is what I came up with.

The protein balls were so good that during football season, Eric made a recurring request to always have these balls handy so he would have the energy and protein to catch his balls.

MAKES ABOUT 16 PROTEIN BALLS

1½ cups old-fashioned rolled oats

1 scoop protein powder of your choice (I like chocolate because it adds more flavor)

½ cup unsweetened creamy peanut butter

⅓ cup pure maple syrup

⅓ cup semisweet chocolate chips

prep time: **35 MINUTES**

IN a large bowl, combine the oats, protein powder, peanut butter, maple syrup, and chocolate chips. Mix together until well incorporated. Cover and refrigerate for at least 30 minutes.

ROLL the mixture into 16 balls, about a heaping tablespoon each, and enjoy. Store in a covered container in the refrigerator for 1 week or in the freezer for 1 month.

Ground Chicken Lettuce Cups

quick feeds

I could drink the sauce from this dish—it's that delicious. The Asian-inspired flavors and the flavorful chicken filling are all wrapped in fresh lettuce, which really helps you forget you're trying to diet.

This is as low-calorie as you can get while still feeling full and enjoying a delicious meal. One tip: Get the reduced-sodium soy sauce.

MAKES 6 SERVINGS

prep time: 10 MINUTES   *cook time:* 15 MINUTES

2 tablespoons olive oil

½ cup diced yellow onion

2 cloves garlic, minced

1 pound ground chicken

Salt and freshly ground black pepper

¼ cup reduced-sodium soy sauce

1 tablespoon Sriracha, or to taste

1 tablespoon cane sugar

1 teaspoon rice vinegar

½ teaspoon grated fresh ginger

6 green leaf lettuce leaves

2 scallions, sliced

IN a large skillet, heat 1 tablespoon of the oil over medium heat. Add the onion and cook until translucent, 3 to 5 minutes. Add the garlic and cook for 1 to 2 minutes, until fragrant.

ADD the ground chicken and cook, breaking up the meat with a wooden spatula as it browns, about 5 minutes. Season with a dash of salt and pepper.

IN a small bowl, whisk together the soy sauce, Sriracha, sugar, vinegar, ginger, and remaining 1 tablespoon oil. Stir the sauce into the meat and let that cook for 3 to 5 minutes to blend the flavors.

FILL each lettuce leaf with a scoop of filling and top with the scallions.

Kid-Friendly

I've been pretty lucky with my little ones when it comes to food. I started them off very young eating what Eric and I ate. We didn't do the whole "Y'all can have mac 'n' cheese from the box and we will have our pork chops and asparagus" thing.

We trained the kids early to eat what we eat and that's final. I raised my little ones to do this because that's how it was at my house growing up. We ate what Mama made and that was that. Now look, I'm not saying it's always easy and that my kids don't ever challenge what I make, because they *do* have their moments.

I also have lots of friends who struggle with getting their kids to eat anything other than what comes in a box, so to help us out a little to get these babies to expand their horizons, I created a full-on chapter of kid-friendly meals that they will eat and you will enjoy, too!

Mac 'n' Cheese

This is as cheesy as it gets! My kids lose their mind over this one. It isn't your typical yellow, creamy mac 'n' cheese. This is like the cheese in the commercials that stretches a mile long. Though mac 'n' cheese usually isn't my favorite, I always dig in to this one.

MAKES 4 TO 6 SERVINGS

prep time: 10 MINUTES   *cook time:* 20 MINUTES

1 pound elbow macaroni

2 tablespoons unsalted butter

1 tablespoon olive oil

3 tablespoons all-purpose flour

1½ cups whole or 2% milk

3 cups shredded white Cheddar cheese

1 cup shredded mozzarella cheese

1 tablespoon garlic powder

Tony Chachere's Creole Seasoning

Salt and freshly ground black pepper

COOK the macaroni until just shy of al dente according to the package directions. Drain and set aside while you make the sauce.

IN a deep skillet, melt the butter with the oil over medium heat for 1 to 2 minutes. Add the flour and stir until smooth, 2 to 3 minutes. Whisk in the milk and gently cook, just to a bubble, until the sauce starts to thicken up, 3 to 5 minutes.

STIR in a handful of each cheese, let them melt together, then repeat until all the cheese is in. Stir in the garlic powder and season with Tony's seasoning and salt and pepper to taste.

FOLD the cooked pasta into the cheese sauce and gently mix until it's all combined.

Maple Syrup Carrots

Carrots and maple syrup—so simple, right? This is a great way to get your kids to eat their veggies. When I was growing up, my aunt Sharon visited us from Australia and made dinner for us and served these carrots. I always disliked carrots as a kid until I had these. Give them a try if your kids aren't carrot fans—they just might change their minds.

MAKES 4 SERVINGS

prep time: 10 MINUTES   *cook time:* 25 MINUTES

3 tablespoons salted butter

3 tablespoons light brown sugar

1 tablespoon pure maple syrup

1 (16-ounce) bag baby carrots

IN a medium saucepan over medium-low heat, melt the butter, brown sugar, and maple syrup, stirring until the sugar is dissolved, about 3 to 4 minutes.

DRAIN the baby carrots and pat dry (if necessary). Add to the saucepan and toss to coat. Cover and let the carrots simmer in the glaze until nice and tender, about 20 minutes.

Sloppy Joes

Mama has been making these since I was a kid. I would always get so excited when I knew these would be for dinner. From the onion to the ground beef with Tony Chachere's spicy seasoning, everything about this recipe makes me happy.

I know maybe you're thinking, a sloppy Joe is a sloppy Joe. I thought the same thing, too, until I tried ordering them in different restaurants and realized how wrong I was. It wasn't like Mama's, and I won't order them out again. This is the best sloppy Joe recipe, and guess what? Kids love it! They are good and slopppppppy. (Billy Madison reference for those who don't know. :))

MAKES 8 SERVINGS

prep time: 5 MINUTES   *cook time:* 25 MINUTES

1 pound ground beef

1 medium onion, diced

1 cup ketchup

1 tablespoon yellow mustard

1 tablespoon light brown sugar

1 tablespoon Worcestershire sauce

½ teaspoon garlic powder

½ teaspoon onion powder

Tony Chachere's Creole Seasoning

Salt

8 King's Hawaiian buns, for serving

IN a large skillet, cook the beef over medium heat, breaking it up with a wooden spoon, until browned, 5 to 7 minutes. Drain off the fat.

ADD in the onion, then stir in the ketchup, mustard, brown sugar, and Worcestershire sauce. Stir in the garlic powder and onion powder and season with Tony's seasoning and salt to taste. Bring to a boil over high heat, then reduce to medium-low, cover, and simmer for 15 to 20 minutes to blend the flavors.

SERVE on the Hawaiian buns.

Sweet Potato Fries

I know it sounds crazy, but I actually never had sweet potato fries until about four years ago. I was in New Jersey at another football wife's house while the guys were away for a game. We had our kids playing together and she popped sweet potato fries in the oven with garlic salt. I thought to myself, As adventurous as I am when it comes to food, have I been living under a rock to not have ever eaten sweet potato fries?

Here is my version of sweet potato fries with a little bit more seasoning to spruce up things. The kids love them and so do grown-ups! So, get those fries ready because. . . . when you dip I dip we dip . . . into some ketchup!

MAKES 6 SERVINGS

prep time: 10 MINUTES   *cook time:* 25 MINUTES

2 pounds sweet potatoes, peeled

2 to 4 tablespoons olive oil

1 teaspoon garlic powder

1 teaspoon paprika

1 teaspoon salt

½ teaspoon freshly ground black pepper

PREHEAT the oven to 400°F.

CUT the sweet potatoes into sticks ¼ to ½ inch thick and 3 inches long and lay them out on a baking sheet and drizzle with the olive oil. Season with the garlic powder, paprika, salt, and pepper and toss to coat.

BAKE until browned and crisp on the bottom, about 15 minutes. Flip and cook until the other side is crisp, about 10 minutes. Serve hot.

Varsity Chili Dogs

Chili on a hot dog—are ya kidding me? How does it get better than that!? These are messy (I'm not gonna sugarcoat it), but they are meaty and delicious. Now I know it seems small, but ya can't skip the mustard on the top at the end. It really makes it.

MAKES 6 TO 10 SERVING

FOR THE CHILI SAUCE

1 pound ground beef

1 (8-ounce) can tomato sauce

½ cup ketchup

2 tablespoons yellow mustard

1 tablespoon light brown sugar

½ teaspoon chili powder

½ teaspoon garlic powder

½ teaspoon onion powder

Dash of Worcestershire sauce

Salt and freshly ground black pepper

FOR THE VARSITY DOGS

6 beef hot dogs

6 hot dog buns

Yellow mustard, for serving

prep time: 10 MINUTES   *cook time:* 30 MINUTES

make the chili sauce: In a large saucepan over medium heat, brown the beef until it's no longer pink. Drain off the fat. Stir in the tomato sauce, ketchup, mustard, brown sugar, chili powder, garlic powder, onion powder, Worcestershire sauce, and salt and pepper to taste. Simmer over low heat, uncovered, for 20 minutes to blend the flavors and thicken slightly.

assemble the varsity dogs: Cook the hot dogs according to the package directions. Place a hot dog in a bun and top with chili sauce and yellow mustard.

Strawberry Greek Yogurt Pops

These are so delicious and so easy. But what I love the most is they are so fun to make with your kids. You can order the homemade ice pop handles online or grab them at Target (while you're picking up the ingredients you need to make these) and have a pop party. We like to add the word "party" to the end of everything. Pizza party, popcorn party, ice pop party. I just think it makes everything fun and it feels like a special event with your kids. We will all chant it together in sync! Try it right now with your little ones. Pop party, pop party!

MAKES 8 POPS

prep time: 5 MINUTES, PLUS AT LEAST 4 HOURS TO FREEZE

12 ounces (1½ cups) plain low-fat or fat-free Greek yogurt

3 cups diced fresh or frozen strawberries, plus sliced strawberries (optional) for garnish

¼ cup honey or pure maple syrup

2 tablespoons fresh lemon juice

1 teaspoon pure vanilla extract

IN a high-powered blender or food processor, combine the yogurt, berries, honey, lemon juice, and vanilla and blend until smooth.

PORTION the yogurt mixture into ice pop molds or 3-ounce plastic cups arranged on a baking sheet or large plate. Top your pop with sliced strawberries if desired, then insert pop sticks.

FREEZE for at least 4 hours or overnight before serving.

Banana Bread Muffins

We love banana bread and banana muffins in our house and make both frequently, especially in the fall. I like to bake these in mini muffin tins so they are cute and small and feel like less of a commitment. Melt butter on top as soon as they come out of the oven so the top gets that gooey texture. Because they're mini, I love putting one or two in my kids' lunch boxes as an extra treat.

MAKES 12 MUFFINS

prep time: 10 MINUTES   *cook time:* 20 MINUTES

Cooking spray, for the muffin tin

3 very ripe bananas, mashed

2 large eggs

½ cup pure maple syrup

1 teaspoon vanilla extract

8 tablespoons (1 stick) unsalted butter, melted and cooled

¼ teaspoon ground cinnamon

2 tablespoons light brown sugar

1½ cups all-purpose flour

1 teaspoon baking soda

½ teaspoon Himalayan pink salt

PREHEAT the oven to 350°F. Coat 12 cups of a muffin tin with cooking spray or line with cupcake liners.

IN a large bowl, stir together the bananas, eggs, maple syrup, vanilla, melted butter, cinnamon, and brown sugar. In a separate bowl, whisk together the flour, baking soda, and salt.

ADD the flour mixture to the banana mixture and stir until no streaks of flour remain. Portion the batter into the prepared muffin cups.

BAKE until a toothpick inserted into the center of a muffin comes out clean, 16 to 20 minutes. Move to a wire rack to cool before serving.

Dessert (Saving the Best for Last)

Cakes and cookies and bars, oh my! My goodness, where do I even begin on this one? I love me some sweets, ya'll. Skipping dessert is not even a thing for me. It's as important to me as the appetizer or the main course. I need to finish things off with my sweets to feel totally satisfied. It's silly, but I'm like a little kid in the way that I rush through my main course to get to my little reward: dessert. I had so many dessert recipes that I had to cut some out so they didn't overshadow the other chapters. Maybe I need a dessert cookbook next? OK, let the sweets begin. Turn the page, sweetie . . .

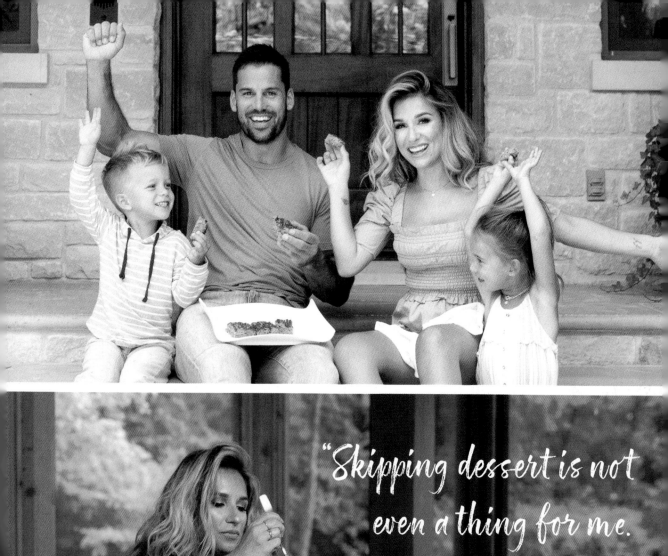

"Skipping dessert is not even a thing for me. It's as important to me as the appetizer or the main course."

Apple Crisp

I started making this apple crisp the first year Eric and I moved in together. I didn't have a ton of experience baking, but I had my mama and our long line of cooks' blood, so I knew if I put my mind to it I would be able to figure it out.

Eric had just started in the NFL and I knew I had a hungry big boy on my hands that I needed to keep fed when he came home from football practice. I also knew he had a sweet tooth and loved apples more than anyone I've ever met. Seriously, the man goes through a bag of apples a week. I never looked up a recipe for this dessert—I just put together what felt right and miraculously it came out perfectly and is still a go-to after all these years.

MAKES 6 SERVINGS

prep time: **15 MINUTES**   *cook time:* **50 MINUTES**

Cooking spray, for the baking dish

6 Golden Delicious apples, peeled and chopped

2 tablespoons granulated sugar

1 teaspoon ground cinnamon

2 teaspoons fresh lemon juice

FOR THE TOPPING

1 cup packed light brown sugar

¾ cup old-fashioned rolled oats

¾ cup all-purpose flour

1 teaspoon ground cinnamon

Pinch of salt

8 tablespoons (1 stick) cold unsalted butter, diced into small cubes

PREHEAT the oven to 350°F. Grease a 9 × 13-inch glass or ceramic baking dish with cooking spray or a little butter.

IN a large bowl, toss the apples with the granulated sugar, cinnamon, and lemon juice.

make the topping: In a medium bowl, whisk together the brown sugar, oats, flour, cinnamon, and salt. Cut the cold butter into the mix and use a pastry cutter or two forks to incorporate.

LAYER the apples in the prepared baking dish and sprinkle the oat mixture over the top. Smooth the topping into an even layer. Bake until the top is golden brown, 40 to 50 minutes. Serve warm. Cover and refrigerate for up to 4 days.

Edible Chocolate Chip Cookie Dough

Cookie dough you can eat without getting sick? Heck yes! Anytime I would make my famous chocolate chip cookies I would always get so frustrated and have to literally hide the cookie dough bowl from Eric because he digs his big fingers into the dough and I'm left with half of the batch gone. I'm partly annoyed because I wanted all two dozen cookies to survive, but I also get a little worried he's going to get a tummy ache from the raw eggs and flour. So I made some edible cookie dough for my sweet-tooth hubby to eat guilt-free! This is such a great recipe and you can freeze half the batch for later.

MAKES 8 TO 10 SERVINGS

prep time: 10 MINUTES   *cook time:* 5 MINUTES

2 cups all-purpose flour

2 sticks (8 ounces) unsalted butter, at room temperature

½ cup cane sugar

1 cup packed light brown sugar

1 teaspoon pure vanilla extract

½ teaspoon sea salt

2 cups semisweet chocolate chips

PREHEAT the oven to 350°F. Line a large baking sheet with parchment paper.

SPREAD the flour evenly on the prepared baking sheet and bake for 8 minutes. Remove from the oven and let cool.

IN a large bowl, with an electric mixer, cream the butter and both sugars until smooth. Stir in the vanilla and salt. Mix in the toasted flour ¼ cup at a time until a soft dough forms. Fold in the chocolate chips. Refrigerate any uneaten cookie dough in a sealed container for up to 3 days.

Can of Cola Cake

The best chocolate cake you will ever have is right here, people. Moist, chocolaty cake and a ganache-like frosting with Coca-Cola in it. I fell in love with this cake when I would frequent one of my favorite restaurants in the South. I decided I needed to have it more frequently and I didn't want to have to rely on hopping into my car to go to the restaurant to enjoy it. Here is as close to the recipe as I could get, since like many places with bomb recipes, they like to keep their recipes top secret—I don't blame 'em! But a girl's gotta have her cake and eat it, too.

MAKES 15 SERVINGS

prep time: 15 MINUTES   *cook time:* 30 MINUTES

FOR THE CAKE

- 8 tablespoons (1 stick) unsalted butter, plus more for the pan
- 2 cups all-purpose flour, plus more for the pan
- 1 cup Coca-Cola
- ½ cup vegetable oil
- 2 cups granulated sugar
- ½ cup buttermilk or ½ cup milk and 1 teaspoon lemon juice
- 2 large eggs
- 2 teaspoons pure vanilla extract
- ¾ cup unsweetened cocoa powder
- 1 teaspoon baking soda

FOR THE FROSTING

- 8 tablespoons (1 stick) unsalted butter
- ½ cup unsweetened cocoa powder
- ¼ cup Coca-Cola, plus more if needed
- ¼ cup chocolate syrup
- 1 teaspoon pure vanilla extract
- 3 cups powdered sugar

make the cake: Preheat the oven to 350°F. Grease and flour a 9 × 13-inch cake pan.

IN a large saucepan over medium heat, combine the Coke, oil, and the 8 tablespoons butter and bring to a boil, 5 to 7 minutes.

MEANWHILE, in a medium bowl, stir together the 2 cups flour and granulated sugar.

WHEN the Coke mixture comes to a boil, stir in the flour mixture and beat. Remove from the heat. Beat in the buttermilk, eggs, vanilla, cocoa powder, and baking soda.

POUR the batter into the prepared pan. Bake until a toothpick inserted in the center comes out clean, about 30 minutes.

meanwhile, make the frosting: In a large bowl, with an electric mixer, cream the butter and cocoa. Beat in the Coke, chocolate syrup, and vanilla. Beat in the powdered sugar ½ cup at a time, scraping down the sides frequently. If the frosting is too stiff, add a little Coke to loosen it.

FROST the cake while it is still warm. Store at room temperature, wrapped tightly with plastic wrap, or in the refrigerator for up to 5 days.

DESSERT (SAVING THE BEST FOR LAST)

Mama's Banana Pudding

It's puddin', not pudding, just to clarify. :) Let me just tell ya, my mama's banana puddin' could win contests, y'all. This is not a box recipe that you can get at the grocery store. This is honest-to-god, made-from-scratch puddin'. What's unique about this (other than the obvious) is that you serve it warm, not cold like we've all been trained to think about banana pudding. The reason it's served warm is because when my mama was little and her mama would make it, she would get so impatient and not want to wait for it to cool that she would dig in right then and there while it was still warm. She realized it was much better that way and I completely agree. This recipe is as unique as it is simple, and even made from scratch. You don't have to use box mixes to make things easy!

MAKES 6 TO 8 SERVINGS

prep time: 10 MINUTES   *cook time:* 10 MINUTES

¾ cup sugar

3 tablespoons cornstarch

¼ teaspoon salt

2 cups whole milk

2 egg yolks, lightly beaten

1½ teaspoons pure vanilla
  extract

1 (11-ounce) box Nilla wafers

2 to 3 bananas, sliced into
  ½-inch-thick rounds

IN a medium saucepan, combine the sugar, cornstarch, and salt. Set the pan over medium heat and gradually pour in the milk, whisking until smooth. Add the egg yolks and slowly bring the mixture to a boil. Cook until the pudding begins to thicken, about 2 minutes. Remove from the heat and stir in the vanilla. Let the pudding set at room temperature for 10 minutes, or until the pudding is no longer hot but still warm.

PLACE a layer of the wafers in the bottom of a clear serving bowl or trifle dish. Top with the warm pudding, followed by a layer of sliced bananas. Repeat the layering until the pudding is gone.

TOP with crushed or broken wafers and serve warm. Refrigerate leftovers for up to three days.

Olive Oil Cake

I went to a restaurant a few years ago that had all these interesting tapas (which I love because of the variety of flavors all at once) and I got so full that I could not even think about dessert. Well, they brought the dessert menu over anyway and of course I had to skim it just to see if something piqued my interest, and I saw the words "olive oil cake." I thought to myself, This could be really amazing, or this could be totally weird. I never had olive oil in my dessert before, but I'm extremely adventurous when it comes to food so I just had to order it out of plain darn curiosity.

All I can remember after that first bite is that I went into panic mode because I was so worried Eric was going to try it and I was going to have to share it with him. Well, he did try it, and it was so good that we fought over the last bite. I couldn't forget that delicious olive oil cake, so I came home and did as much research as possible. This recipe is what I came up with. It is so moist and has the perfect amount of sweet and tart with the apricot syrup.

MAKES 8 SERVINGS

prep time: 10 MINUTES   *cook time:* 1 HOUR

FOR THE CAKE

Cooking spray, for the
  cake pan
2½ cups sugar
4 large eggs
2½ cups extra-virgin olive oil
¾ cup heavy cream
¾ cup whole milk
½ teaspoon pure vanilla
  extract
½ teaspoon almond extract
2½ cups all-purpose flour
1¼ teaspoons kosher salt
½ teaspoon baking soda
½ teaspoon baking powder

make the cake: Preheat the oven to 300°F. Coat an 8-inch cake pan with cooking spray.

IN a large bowl, with an electric mixer or a whisk, beat the sugar and eggs until pale. Beat in the olive oil, cream, and milk and then the vanilla and almond extract.

IN a separate large bowl, whisk together the flour, salt, baking soda, and baking powder.

ADD half of the dry ingredients to the wet and mix well. Then add the remaining dry mixture and stir until there are no lumps.

POUR the batter into the prepared pan and bake until a toothpick inserted in the center comes out clean, about 45 minutes.

FOR THE SYRUP

1 cup sugar

2 tablespoons apricot preserves

1 tablespoon grated lemon zest

make the syrup: In a small saucepan, combine 1½ cups water, the sugar, apricot preserves, and lemon zest. Bring to a boil over medium heat and stir until the sugar is dissolved. Reduce the heat to medium-low and cook until the syrup thickens, 10 to 15 minutes. Remove from the heat.

WHEN the cake is finished, poke holes with a skewer or knife throughout the cake. Drizzle with the apricot syrup. Store in an airtight container at room temperature or in the refrigerator for up to 5 days.

Oatmeal Chocolate Chip Cookies

A couple of years ago I discovered that I had a slight allergy to oats, which was truly devastating. I'm lucky that it's not too serious (I just get an upset stomach), but I was still so sad to have to start avoiding one of my all-time favorite ingredients. I have been in love with oats for as long as I can remember. My favorite breakfast was those little packets of strawberry oatmeal and water and a little splash of milk when it came out of the microwave. My kids absolutely love oatmeal as well. It is a part of their morning routine. I don't know why I developed this allergy, but I think I just went overkill with oats over the years and sometimes after babies your body can develop new sensitivities.

Well, now I know you're wondering why I am so excited about these oatmeal chocolate chip cookies, since I'm slightly allergic. Believe it or not, these oatmeal chocolate chip cookies are that darn good that I sacrifice a stomachache just so I can have them! For those who don't have an allergy or aversion to oats, dig in! One is not enough. I love to dip these in milk for dessert, or even for breakfast.

MAKES ABOUT 18 COOKIES

prep time: 5 MINUTES   *cook time:* 7 TO 9 MINUTES

½ cup coconut oil, melted

½ cup packed light brown sugar

¼ cup granulated sugar

1 teaspoon ground cinnamon

¼ teaspoon sea salt

1 large egg

1½ tablespoons pure vanilla extract

1 cup old-fashioned rolled oats

1 cup all-purpose flour

1 teaspoon baking soda

1 cup semisweet chocolate chips

PREHEAT the oven to 350°F. Line a baking sheet with parchment paper.

IN a large bowl, whisk together the coconut oil, brown sugar, granulated sugar, cinnamon, salt, egg, and vanilla. Stir in the oats, flour, and baking soda until a dough forms. Fold in the chocolate chips.

SCOOP 1 heaping tablespoon of dough for each cookie and form it into a ball. Working in batches, arrange on the prepared baking sheet with a little space for the cookies to spread. To prevent too much spreading, you can chill the dough after it's scooped and then pop it in the oven!

BAKE until the edges begin to brown and crisp, about 8 minutes. Repeat with the remaining dough.

COOL the cookies slightly before moving them to a wire rack to cool completely.

PLACE on a pretty platter and watch the hands make their way to these delicious treats. Store in an airtight container at room temperature for 3 to 5 days.

Pumpkin Chocolate Chip Cookies

One of my good girlfriends in Denver, Colorado, made me pumpkin chocolate chip cookies and I will never forget it. This truly was the first time I had ever had pumpkin chocolate chip cookies, which is now so crazy to think about since I have been obsessed with chocolate chip cookies my entire life, so why didn't I think to add the pumpkin?

Well, now I have, and here is the recipe that I make every single fall. I get so excited around the time of year when they start putting out cans of pumpkin puree at the grocery store that I always buy way too many. I just don't want to run out because at any moment I need to be ready to make these amazing pumpkin chocolate chip cookies. Just a warning: When you make these cookies and they come out of the oven, you may possibly try to eat the entire batch.

MAKES 18 COOKIES

prep time: 5 MINUTES   *cook time:* 10 MINUTES

1 cup canned unsweetened
   pumpkin puree

1 cup sugar

½ cup canola or vegetable oil

2 teaspoons pure vanilla
   extract

1 teaspoon milk

1 large egg

2 cups all-purpose flour

2 teaspoons baking powder

1 teaspoon baking soda

1 teaspoon ground cinnamon

½ teaspoon salt

1½ cups semisweet chocolate
   chips

PREHEAT the oven to 375°F. Line a baking sheet with parchment paper or coat with cooking spray.

IN a large bowl, stir together the pumpkin puree, sugar, oil, vanilla, milk, and egg. In a separate bowl, whisk together the flour, baking powder, baking soda, cinnamon, and salt. Add the flour mixture to the pumpkin mixture and mix until a soft dough forms. Fold in the chocolate chips.

WORKING in batches, scoop spoonfuls of dough onto the prepared pan and smooth over any rough edges. I like mine bite-size to be able to fit in the palm of my hand.

BAKE until the cookies just begin to brown, about 10 minutes. Repeat with the remaining dough.

COOL cookies slightly before moving them to a wire rack to cool completely. Store in an airtight container at room temperature for 3 to 5 days.

Yankee Bars

My husband, Eric, grew up in Minnesota, and I have learned over the years that Minnesota has its own style of food and secret recipes that only people from the North would know about. One of them is dessert bars. I never had bars growing up; it was mostly peach cobbler or chocolate chip cookies. But after a few years into our relationship and him constantly expressing that he wanted me to make him bars like he grew up with, I decided to do my research! Cornflakes, peanut butter, and sugar? Count me in! This is what I came up with and I am happy to say that even though the "bar" was high . . . I passed the test. Here are what I now call Yankee Bars.

MAKES 16 SQUARES

prep time: 5 MINUTES   *cook time:* 10 MINUTES

Cooking spray, for the pan
1 cup creamy peanut butter
½ cup sugar
½ cup light corn syrup
2 cups cornflakes
1⅓ cups chocolate chips

LINE an 8 × 8-inch pan with foil and lightly coat with cooking spray.

IN a medium saucepan, heat the peanut butter, sugar, and corn syrup over low heat to melt, 5 to 7 minutes. Add the cornflakes to a plastic bag and crush them with a rolling pin or a heavy glass. Stir into the peanut butter mixture.

PAT into the prepared pan.

MELT the chocolate chips over low heat and spread over the top. Cool until firm, then cut into 16 squares. Store in an airtight container at room temperature for 3 to 5 days.

Peanut Butter Cookies

These are the most amazing peanut butter cookies you will ever have in your life. I pride myself on being a cookie connoisseur, so when I tell you a cookie is good, I mean it! It took me a while to get this recipe straight, but I think the coconut sugar makes these a real standout in the peanut butter cookie world. They are gooey in the middle and they have a slight crunch around the edges.

What else could ya ask for in a cookie?

MAKES 24 TO 26 COOKIES

prep time: 10 MINUTES   *cook time:* 8 MINUTES

8 tablespoons (1 stick) unsalted butter, at room temperature

½ cup crunchy peanut butter

1 cup coconut sugar

1 large egg

½ tablespoon pure vanilla extract

1½ cups all-purpose flour

¾ teaspoon baking soda

Pinch of fine sea salt

Flaky sea salt, for sprinkling

PREHEAT the oven to 350°F. Line a baking sheet with parchment paper.

IN a large bowl, with an electric mixer or by hand, cream together the butter, peanut butter, coconut sugar, egg, and vanilla. In a separate bowl, whisk together the flour, baking soda, and fine sea salt. Add the flour mixture to the peanut butter mixture and stir well.

WORKING in batches, scoop the dough into balls, 1 to 2 tablespoons each, and place on the prepared baking sheet. Gently press each dough ball with the tines of a fork in a crosshatch pattern.

BAKE until the edges begin to lightly brown, about 8 minutes. Sprinkle with flaky sea salt and let cool. Repeat with the remaining dough.

COOL the cookies slightly before moving them to a wire rack to cool completely. Store in an airtight container at room temperature for 3 to 5 days.

Chocolate Chip Cookies

I know this one was in the last book, but it was too darn good not to include it again. Now you can have your favorite cookie recipes together in one book to make things easier.

MAKES 36 COOKIES

prep time: 5 MINUTES   *cook time:* 10 MINUTES

1 cup grass-fed butter, softened, plus more for the baking sheet

2½ cups all-purpose flour

1 teaspoon baking soda

1 teaspoon salt

½ cup cane sugar

1 cup light brown sugar

1 teaspoon Himalayan pink salt

2 teaspoons pure vanilla extract

2 large eggs

2 cups semisweet chocolate chips

PREHEAT the oven to 375°F. Prepare a baking sheet by rubbing it with butter.

COMBINE the flour, baking soda, and salt in a large bowl.

BEAT the butter, cane sugar, brown sugar, Himalayan pink salt, and vanilla in a large bowl until creamy.

ADD the eggs, one at a time, beating well after each addition. Pour slowly into the flour mixture. Next, throw in the chocolate chips.

WORKING in batches, scoop the dough onto the prepared baking sheet, then bake for about 10 minutes, or until golden brown.

COOL the cookies on the baking sheet for a couple of minutes, but not so long that the cookies continue to bake. Repeat with the remaining dough.

PLACE the cookies on a pretty platter and enjoy! Store in an airtight container at room temperature for 3 to 5 days.

It's Cocktail Time

Sip and enjoy, honey! Here are a few drink recipes from my party to yours.

Skinny Margs

Eric and I love going to Cabo. It's our favorite place to relax and vacation together and really recharge our love batteries. One night we went to a local bar and I saw a few people all drinking the same thing, so I asked the bartender what it was. He listed the ingredients and it was like a skinnier version of a margarita! We loved it so much I decided to make our own at home from memory.

MAKES 4 DRINKS

prep time: 15 MINUTES

Coarse salt, for the rims (optional)

Ice

½ cup tequila

Juice of 2 limes

1 to 2 teaspoons agave

IF desired, rim 4 pretty glasses with salt. In an ice-filled cocktail shaker, combine the tequila, lime juice, and agave and shake it up. Fill the glasses with ice and strain the margaritas into them. Add the squeezed limes to the glass for presentation and that extra "twist."

Mermaid Juice

My sister Sydney threw me a stunning mermaid-themed bridal shower because I am obsessed with mermaids and everyone in my life knows it. She created a "mermaid punch" as the signature drink for everyone to enjoy at the shower. I don't think anyone even realized there was alcohol in it . . . it's that good!

The colors are so pretty and festive and it's perfect for any summer occasion. It would even be a beautiful drink to serve (without the alcohol) at a boy's baby shower!

MAKES 4 DRINKS

2 cups ice
¼ cup blue Curaçao
1 cup white rum
2 cups lemonade
1 liter ginger ale
4 lemon wheels
8 maraschino cherries

prep time: 10 MINUTES

PUT ¼ cup ice in each hurricane glass, then add the liquids in this order: 1 tablespoon blue Curaçao, ¼ cup rum, another ¼ cup ice (the ice helps with the ombré effect), ½ cup lemonade, and a quarter of the ginger ale.

SET a lemon wheel on each rim and garnish with the maraschino cherries.

Christmas Punch

I was looking for something fragrant to fill up the house on Christmas morning and I came across a recipe similar to this. Let me tell ya, this is a hit!

MAKES 8 SERVINGS

prep time: 5 MINUTES   *cook time:* 20 MINUTES

½ gallon apple cider

1½ cups cranberries, plus more for garnish

2 oranges, sliced

3 sprigs fresh rosemary

3 or 4 cinnamon sticks

Ice

1 (750-ml) bottle Champagne, chilled

IN a large saucepan, combine the apple cider, 4 cups water, the cranberries, orange slices, rosemary, and cinnamon and simmer over medium-low heat for 20 minutes, which will fill the room with cinnamon fragrance.

LET cool, then ladle into wineglasses over ice and top with Champagne to serve.

Rum-Away Frozen Goodness

It was a hot day on vacation in Florida when we wanted something frozen and good and no one had a piña colada mix or tequila. I looked around in the kitchen to see what we had and threw it all together. Let me tell you it was a pleasant surprise and everyone fell in love. Between the fresh taste of lime and the subtle taste of icy sweet rum, this drink is like a vacation in a cup. Never forget this has alcohol; so drink slowly!

SERVES 3

prep time: 5 MINUTES

2 cups ice

1 (12-ounce) can ginger ale
  (I like Zevia)

1 cup rum

1 tablespoon pure maple syrup

1 lime

FILL a blender with the ice. Add the ginger ale, rum, and maple syrup. Squeeze the lime juice into the blender, and then throw in the remainder of the lime with the peel. Blend until smooth.

SERVE in pretty cups.

The Last Bite

I hope y'all enjoyed my very first cookbook. This was one of the most exciting things I've ever done because I got to write and think and talk about food for months and months as I created *Just Feed Me*.

If you are not a big cook or didn't grow up cooking but really want to learn, I hope that my recipes made you feel like you could create anything, and that cooking doesn't have to be intimidating. It's all about making something that feeds your soul and family and it doesn't matter how we get there, complicated or simple: Just feed me, baby!

I pride myself in being unafraid to try anything at least once when it comes to cookin'! I've always been a believer that you can do whatever you put your mind to, and it's OK if we mess up things and have to try again. I have thrown out many things that didn't come out right and I just tried again until I got them right. I have this little sign I keep on my stovetop that says, "Good moms have sticky floors, dirty ovens, and happy kids." I love that sign because it could not be more reflective of our kitchen and home. We do what we can in our own special way, and that's what makes life beautiful.

I hope y'all continue to join me, roll up your sleeves, and get your hands dirty in the kitchen! I truly enjoyed making this book and I look forward to seeing your pictures of your favorite recipes and meals. From my kitchen to yours, "Just feed me!"

Acknowledgments

I want to thank my amazing team at HarperCollins for believing in me and supporting my dream to write my very first cookbook! Lisa Sharkey, for being my cheerleader and helping me make this project happen. Matt Harper, for his patience and staying on top of me to get my book finished on time (LOL). Also at HarperCollins a huge thank-you to Anna Montague, Maddie Pillari, Rachel Meyers, Michelle Crowe, Julie Paulauski, and Kendra Newton.

I want to thank the talented Liz Schoch for helping to bring my food to life through her beautiful photos and styling.

I also want to thank my amazing agents Sloane and Margaret at WME for being my badass squad and supporting me through this entire process.

Thank you to the amazing team and photographers, John Hillin and Liz Schoch, who helped put this together.

Index

About the Author

Singer-songwriter, TV personality, fashion mogul, beauty and lifestyle influencer/entrepreneur, and *New York Times* bestselling author Jessie James Decker has emerged as a multiplatform juggernaut, juggling fashion brands like her personally founded and created brand Kittenish—with two retail stores and growing—and popular boot and sunglasses lines, along with her television-hosting duties. Jessie's passion for music has made the multitalented Warner Music Nashville artist one of music's true breakout firebrands. On her 2009 self-title debut, the singer's authentic style immediately captivated listeners everywhere. She continued to keep it real with her second studio album, 2017's *Southern Girl City Lights*, which debuted at No. 1 on Billboard's Top Country Albums chart. Jessie lives with her husband, retired NFL player Eric Decker, and their three children in Nashville, Tennessee.